Christopher

Chief Petty Officer RN (Rtd)

Illustrations, design and typeset

by

Michelle (Shelly) Turner

www.carboncopyarts.com | carboncopyarts@gmail.com

Printed in Great Britain by 4edge 2018

ISBN 978-0 9927601-1-3

Order Form can be obtained online from

warandpeaceybook@gmail.com

Book can be purchased from Amazon.

From the author of

IF YOU CAN'T TAKE A JOKE.... YOU SHOULDN'T HAVE JOINED

Acknowledgements

Chris. Peacey. For your service to our country, for our friendship, and for the fun we have had when drilling down into your past; for us to put some of those stored away memories onto paper and into some sort of order.

Sheila Penney. Your support, encouragement and your god given wisdom has been vital.

Michelle 'Shelly' Turner, multi-talented and highly efficient, your design, typeset and illustrations have brought this book to life, and have portrayed those humorous incidents that were etched in Chris's memory bank.

Roger Alldred, for the provision of excellent photographs for `Shelly' to work with.

David Hallett, and all at 4edge Limited of Hockley Essex, for production advice and for the book's superb finish.

To my wife Jan, being supportive and patient, as always.

My thanks to Malcolm (Dobbo) Dobson of the HMS Decoy Association (dobbo.exrn@btinternet.com) also, to Dennis Andrew of the HMS Tiger Association. The book has been reviewed by Dick Lloyd, editor of the HMS Ganges Association Gazette, for and on behalf of the association members. I am grateful to Paul and Jan Dawson and those others too numerous to mention here, for efforts in aid of Combat Stress.

DEAR MARTIN
BEST REGARDS
Bob Clark

War and Peacey

I was one of the lucky ones! I came through the long and
brutal war physically and mentally unscathed, even though at
times death and destruction was happening around me. As
you will read in this book, events occurred which even today
play on my mind and sometimes cause me nightmares.
I often wondered about those wounded shattered men; those
injured during the bombing and sinking of the ships and
those we had brought back from the invasion beachheads.
After they had been stretched ashore my last sight of them
would be as the doors of those waiting military ambulances
were being closed. But for those men and for their families it
was the opening of a new chapter in their lives. My hope was
that wherever those men were taken to could provide the
long-term care many of them would now need
It is for those reasons I want to donate from this book to the
charity 'Combat Stress' whose aim is to support Veterans
with mental health problems.

In support of

COMBAT
STRESS

FOR VETERANS' MENTAL HEALTH

The Good Old Days

Hi Bob.

Reference to our chat (BANK HOLIDAY MONDAY) I enclose chq as requested & I'm looking forward to a good read of your book! If you're ever this way – with time to spare you're welcome to call in

Sincerely Yours

Tracey (CHRIS)

Since writing a book which detailed my naval service as a boy seaman undergoing training, and with life as I experienced it aboard a large warship, as well as my service in submarines during the cold war years, I had received many letters such this one shown above.

Often, they had been sent by either serving or retired navy-men who ranked from Admiral, down to those of basic level. They were usually sent in response to reviews of my book, as published in service magazines and association newsletters. If that letter they sent included a phone number, I would ring to thank whoever had ordered the book, and also to learn about their service, which ships or submarines they had served on, and their own experiences. Chris was one of those I spoke to.

He lives at Gosport close to the parish church, and more importantly to Chris, close to the slipway from where in days past he used to launch his boat into the Solent. I was due to attend a function at the Gosport submarine base HMS Dolphin, so I called in to meet Chris at his home before that happened. I was amazed when eventually I discovered that this smart, spritely and humorous man was 90 years of age. Since that first meeting I have visited him many times and have stayed at his home on a number of occasions, and it wasn't long before he would be telling me when it was my turn to make the tea, and of course that is the moment you really know you are welcome. He is a charming host and a pleasant companion who still enjoys a good meal and the occasional pint. Together we have visited some of his old haunts, including the Hardway, a place with conflicting wartime memories for him.

It transpired that he had really enjoyed reading my book but when eventually I heard of his service-record, my own experiences paled into insignificance when compared to his. At his home over a glass of rum, our conversation would cover many topics. We watched a news-report one evening which featured some supporters of Brexit; their reason was to return to 'those good old days'. In response to which I said that I actually couldn't remember when those days were but they probably meant back in 1065, a year before those Norman 'illegal immigrants' came in, but that was before even you were born Chris. Chris then explained that he was raised during that depression following the first war, and those lean days building up to, during, and after the second war. (I think that was the moment when I first realised his age). We did both agree that things got better years later during the 1970s and 1980s; but, of course, we were in the EU by then. We both hoped that those ardent Brexiteers would turn out to be right and would lead us to the land of milk and honey. Chris said he knew he wouldn't be around to find out. "I doubt that I will be either Chris", said I.

As the warming rum took effect, we would compare the navy we had served in with that of today and talk about its diminished role since the war. It has mainly become an anti-submarine force, and since 1968, could no longer afford a role east of Suez. No longer does Britannia 'rule the waves'. She can now only operate within a strike force, in defence of the US Navy's aircraft carriers. I told Chris I would take him to see the first of our two aircraft carriers Queen Elizabeth when she entered Portsmouth (which I have now done) and would do the same when the second, Prince of Wales, followed a year or so later. We both hoped that 'they' could recruit enough of the specialists required to man at least one of the two ships, and then get some aircraft to fly from her - even if some of them are French.

Gradually during our conversations I got him to open up about his own life and service experience, and this is what he told me.............

Keep Whistling Son

I was born June 8th 1924 at my parent's home in the small hamlet of Bulley which sprawls around a few lanes about a mile north of the A40 Gloucester to Ross-on-Wye road and lies in the rolling fertile countryside, five miles as the crow flies to the west of the City of Gloucester. During my early years I thought that Gloucester was the centre of the world and found that as we couldn't travel as the crow does the infrequent, rickety old buses, would take about an hour. Once I was old enough to cycle, keeping clear of the main roads the road mileage would be about eight miles.

We lived in one of two compact adjoining cottages which my parents rented from the owners of the smallholding on which they were set.

My father, William Christopher Peacey known to all as Bill, was a rugged six-footer. He didn't marry until he was over fifty. A pleasant even-tempered man he worked long hard hours, six days a week, track laying and maintenance for the Great Western Railway Company. After World War one, times were hard for the GWR and for the country as a whole due to the depression. During 1929 the 'Development Loans Act' was passed to help stimulate employment and aid growth; rail-track would now be laid, creating new lines, and updating the older ones. Dad worked under a 'ganger' as the foreman was known and they were based at Oakle Street railway halt only a mile away from our home, and that is where their equipment was stored. How they all met up at the location they would work I don't know, as none of the others lived close by, or had telephones, so I assume they would have to cycle. I can remember many times dad getting up in the early hours to place fog warning lights on the tracks before the morning trains were due. He would perhaps say 'there's a racehorse due to come through at five' (that was his term for a streamlined express), another time he would perhaps say 'a couple of carthorses will be working between Ross and Gloucester' (this was how he termed the pannier-style light goods and shunting engines). The 'cob' and 'mechanical horse' were lorries that worked out of the station-yard. I think some of this has rubbed off on me, as throughout my life I also tend to link the mechanical and inanimate creations of mankind to animals, even though like my father before me, I never worked on a farm or with animals. Achingly tired, as often he was, he never lost his temper with me even when I would help myself to his cider which he kept stored in a big forty-gallon oak barrel above the coal and wood-pile in the outhouse.

Late autumn the cider would be delivered by horse and cart from the fruit farm adjacent to Bulley church. The farm is still there to this day producing cider from the same orchards. I would fill up his barrel by taking bucket-loads from the back of the cart. The cider would last him most of the winter. I can still remember mother putting down a drink and some tit-bits for the cart horse, a grey mare by the name of Violet.

Late evenings, seated by the fire, dad would pass me a jug to fill up with cider and I would go out, whatever the weather, to the outhouse. He would say 'keep whistling son' as he knew all the time I was whistling I wasn't drinking his cider. I developed quite a liking for the golden nectar and used to tap off a few pints for myself while he was out at work. When stocks were getting a bit low I'd replace with a little water. My tolerance for alcohol was to stand me in good stead, later in life, when I joined the hard- drinking man's world of the navy.

With my help, dad made wine from anything surplus in the garden, rhubarb, turnips and parsnips. Mum and I gathered greengages, sloes, elder flowers, blackberries and rosehips from which dad made wine, and she made chutney or jam. I learnt how to snare rabbits, and these, along with fish and eels from the River Severn which flowed close by, gave us a healthy and wholesome diet. Upon joining the Navy, I met boys from the cities, many of whom wouldn't know how to feed themselves without their local shops.

Times were pretty hard but we always had coal for heat and enough to barter with, or to give to less fortunate neighbours as dad had a coal allowance from the railway, and if we needed more, the locomotive fireman would shovel some off at a convenient place in exchange for some fruit or vegetables from my dad.

How dad met my mother, Alice Maud, I don't know. She came from the area of Blunsdon, on the northern outskirts of Swindon, which of course had major workshops for the GWR and many of the main line locomotives, finished in their 'Brunswick Green' paint, were built there. Perhaps my father had to work in that area at some time.

Alice Maud was a widow with two sons and a daughter to support, before marrying my father. Her earlier life I know nothing about, but perhaps her widowhood was caused by the war. She worked as a cook, and as they say 'the way to a man's heart is through his stomach', that, coupled with her good looks and kind nature, must have been a great attraction for dad. I knew my mother to be a person who would help any other family less fortunate than ours, and although small in stature, she had great stamina and drive. Dad was a strong, hardworking man but she 'ruled the roost'.

I think I inherited both size and stamina from her but I'm not sure about the good looks!

They were married at Bulley church. I'm sure my dad must have been hoping for a child because from an early age I always felt wanted by both of them. My two half-brothers were much older than me and I rarely saw either of them. David, the eldest, worked as a barman at the Golden Lion, a pub in Ipswich, the younger one, William George (we called him George) served in the air force at Larkhill. I occasionally used George's bike which he kept at our house, he wanted me to buy it but I don't know how he thought I could as I didn't even have a paper-round at that time. He certainly didn't inherit his nature from our mother. My half-sister Catherine lived with us, the few cuffs I got from mum was when Catherine told tales about things we boys got up to. Being the only youngster in my house was not a problem for me. Mr and Mrs Etheridge, who lived next door, had five children, Bill, Kath, Jim, Florence and Denis, so I was never short of playmates. Jim was my age, and we started school at the same time when we were five. We would walk together, there and back, the distance about three miles across fields and along lanes to the Huntley Church School. It was basically one large hall, with a small adjoining room for the primary class. Headmistress, Miss Rogers, a stern woman, had four other female teachers to support her and all of them seemed to be equally stern. After leaving the primary class, we would progress each year, in classes, up the length of the hall, like the seven steps to heaven, before leaving school at the age of fourteen. Some had ambition to be the brightest pupil and be kept on for an extra year as teaching assistant, but not me! We used chalk on slate-boards to practise our writing and to work out sums, copied from the main blackboard. I can remember often being chastised and punished for squeaking my chalk on the board after being told not to. I think it set Miss Cook's teeth on edge. I soon learnt to read, which opened up a whole new world for me, and I have been an avid reader to this day. It pleased my dad. He would be retiring at age sixty-five and had ambition to have a smallholding for us to be self-sufficient as a family. He had already bought a cow to provide some milk for us; she grazed the small grass area behind our home which was a plot large enough to keep a few more animals, as well as the cow. Now that I could read, dad would send me to the livestock auction where I would scan the lists to gain knowledge of current prices, for sheep, goats, chickens and for implements; those items needed to build his dream.

Before having the cow, I would walk a mile to the dairy to fill mum's milk pail, fresh from the cow, not pasteurised. Often it was before I went to school so we could have milk to mash our breakfast oats in. I remember one Saturday morning while walking back with Jim, I was swinging the pail by its handle to show him that centrifugal force would keep the milk from flying out, when suddenly the demonstration went badly wrong, on its downward swing the pail hit the fence, spilling most of the creamy milk over me. The cuff I got from mum didn't hurt me as much as did the laughter I could hear through the wall, as next door to us Jim related the story to his brothers and sisters.

The thin adjoining wall had some advantages. The Etheridge family owned an accumulator-powered wireless; listening to music, BBC news and other programmes, was a link to the outside world. My parents bought the Daily Express newspaper which was delivered by the village paperboy, but its news was usually a day or two old.

I haven't explained before that our cottage, like all others in Bulley, had no electricity, gas or running water. We used oil lamps and candles as lighting. I had come by an old accumulator, from which I powered a car headlamp bulb which I used for reading and for school-homework. Our water came from a two-foot deep well which was behind the cottage which adjoined ours. We would kneel down and scoop it up by using a bucket. It was good drinking water and the well never dried up even during long hot summers, and I can never remember it freezing during a hard winter. Mother would boil the kettle for tea or to fill the tin bath on the coal fired oven range, which was alongside the open fire hearth.

The local butcher came round in his van every Friday. A large beef joint, complete with bones, would provide roast on Sunday and a few other meals during the week. Mum would boil the bones and add vegetables for soup. Sometimes the meat would be mutton, tasty and quite plentiful in our area. The baker came all the way from Gloucester by van, on his delivery-round. That bread lasted us most of the week, but, as he also supplied the baker's shop at Huntley we would buy a loaf from there if we needed to. I never had hunger that couldn't be satisfied, nor had sickness from rotten food. Without refrigeration and with just a larder, mother kept everything shielded from flies and other insects which were abundant in those days.

He was the centre of attraction for the ladies

With other boys of my age, or thereabouts, I sang in a choir run by the local parson, not because we were devout in the religious sense, but it gave us boys a chance to get together and have a bit of fun once we were out of public view. We sang at three local churches each Sunday. Bulley church, known as the 'church amid the trees' is a really beautiful Norman church built on Saxon foundations, Huntley church which stands close to my school, and the Birdwood Mission. One Sunday while singing at Huntley church, I noticed a local farmer, his wife and their son in the congregation. The son, who was on leave from the Navy, was smartly dressed in his naval uniform-clothing. He was the centre of attraction for the ladies and also a point of interest for the men because most of them had never been outside of Gloucestershire. I think a seed was sown inside me. I had no desire to work on the land or with animals. Around this time, I had a bad experience that affected my love of horses.

Jim and I would pass a mare on our way to school, she would come to the paddock gate and put her head down to take fresh grass from our hands and was happy for us to pat and stroke her. She was gone from the paddock for a week, and then the following Saturday I was pleased to see her at the far side of the paddock with her spindly legged foal standing next to her. She wouldn't come to the gate so I plucked some grass, climbed the gate, and walked towards her. Suddenly, she reared up, let out a fearsome whinnying and charged me.

Even now, all these years later, in my mind's eye I can picture
her with her tail and mane swirling as I turned back and ran.
How I got over that gate and avoided her flailing hooves I
don't know. I was shaking all over, and from that day I have
never trusted horses completely. I knew local farm boys who
had been trampled by their cows, and one who was gored by
a bull, others who suffered accidents using farm machinery.
Quite often they worked alone, in bad light and in whatever
weather nature offered, not at all like Old McDonald's farm.
Many years later, I was sad to hear that my school-friend Jim

had contracted tuberculosis from cows at the farm he worked on, causing him to die while in his mid-thirties.

Like most lads, Jim and I had a passion for cars and motor cycles. We would walk up to the main road and sit on the stone wall at the verge, to spot the different models of cars and of the lorries that came by. Traffic was sporadic, even the A40 had long gaps, as few families would own a car. Every make had distinct lines and we knew their different badges and logos. Jim's favourite make was the Jaguar and mine the MG, we both vowed that one day we would each own one of our favoured models. It was twenty years before I made good on that vow, but unfortunately I don't think Jim was able to.

One day we spoke with an AA patrolman who had parked his motor cycle sidecar-unit near the spot we usually sat. He would pause during his conversation with us to salute any car sporting the AA emblem that passed by. His mention of motor garages in Gloucester which would offer boys of school leaving age apprenticeship, sowed another seed in my young brain.

I was only twelve years old when my whole world fell apart. Dad was within a week of retirement and was ready to set up his long held ambition to have a smallholding, when he suddenly died, right in front of me, while in our living room. I cannot describe the grief and emptiness that I felt. Life at home would never be the same for me, or for my mother, who was now a widow for the second time. We had to survive on the small pension from the GWR and without the love and support of that truly great man. I grew up fast and had to try and become the man of the house. I couldn't concentrate at school and withdrew into my own world.

I now rode to school on an old cycle that I had been given, which saved precious time, because after school I needed to tend our garden, from which much of our food came.

One thundery summer's day I was pedalling towards school with my head down into the wind, when, with a blinding flash lightning struck the handlebars, throwing me from the bike into the ditch. I was either concussed by the lightning or by contact with the ground. Awakening from my daze, I gradually re-focused my eyesight. The bike had blue-black scorch marks on the handlebars but otherwise was intact and went on to serve me well. We boys usually rode upright with our hands on the bars, close to the head. Because of the headwinds on that occasion I rode bent over, with my hands on the rubber grips. I am sure my life was saved be me taking that action. Many are the times throughout my life when some 'being' seemed to be watching over me.

Catherine left home to work 'in service' as a housemaid at a large country estate. I rarely saw her after then, because I was away in the Navy when she returned home. I was still away when she left home to marry and to live elsewhere in Gloucestershire. She died at age seventy-two and is buried at Bulley church, in the same grave as my father and my mother.

I began to realise that I had a knack of fixing things mechanical. I mended things around the home and was called on to fix other people's bikes. Mother noticed this aptitude and somehow raised sixty pounds to buy a three year apprenticeship for me to work at Westgate Motor House, a Standard Motors agent in Gloucester. I was now approaching fourteen and would soon leave school.

On a warm Monday morning in mid-August 1938 I got up early to set off on my bike for my first work-day. I had made the journey before when I had attended an interview with the foreman, so I had some idea of how long it should take. I allowed extra time, and was there an hour before opening time. I can still remember looking up at the old Gloucester bi-plane that stood on the garage roof, almost overhanging at the front. Mr King the owner of the garage was an air enthusiast, perhaps he had served in the war. From the very start I loved my job, and quickly learnt the basics. Many procedures I could do without supervision, but the foreman was very thorough and a good teacher, he always checked before I completed any task.

At the end of that first year I felt confident as a mechanic, but all the while I was conscious that war with Germany was likely, and I began to think about joining the Navy. Knowing that they took boys at age fifteen, I made an application by post to the recruiting office in Bristol. Soon after the declaration of war in September 1939, I was notified to attend there for a medical examination and other tests. After completion of this I heard nothing and carried on with my work at Westgate Motors. I checked the post daily and waited. I worried that the war would be over before I did my bit, so you can imagine my joy when I arrived home one day to find an envelope which contained my joining orders, and a railway warrant to travel via Bristol, to Ipswich Station in Suffolk. There I would be met and taken to the boy's training establishment HMS Ganges.

I Am Next To God

The country was at war; the period known as 'the phoney war', the date was now 21st November 1939. My train journey took me from Gloucester to Paddington via Bristol. I then crossed London by underground to Liverpool Street station where I boarded the train to Ipswich. This was new and exciting for me, my first time as a passenger on a train. I had watched many times looking over the railway bridge parapet as trains thundered past below. I loved the smell and taste of the steamy, coal smoke mixture. Now I leaned out of the window, as we flashed past sheep and cows in the pasture, and saw farm labourers working the horse-drawn ploughs. All seemed so peaceful and normal, but seeing the uniform-clad men and women in the carriages and on the stations especially through London, was a reminder that the country was mobilising to halt the Nazi war machine.

Ipswich station was busy, mainly with men in naval uniform. One I met said there were some destroyers and motor gun boats based at Harwich. I was directed to join a gathering of lads who were standing alongside their cases. We climbed up, to the back of a blue RN truck and stood, holding on to the metal frames under the canvas covering as it negotiated the country roads to HMS Ganges on the Shotley peninsula.

I had no idea of what to expect and was amazed at the size of Ganges. There were many brick buildings as well as numerous large wooden huts. It was now late evening and almost dark; we were taken to what was to be our dormitory, after having been given a plate of lukewarm fish and chips with a mug of milk. This dormitory would become the home for about thirty of us, during the four weeks we spent as 'nozzers'; the term for new entries. The food, and the old metal plate it was served on, was a rude awakening for me, and I came to realise how good a cook mother was, how tasty and flavoursome her meals with all the good garden and field fare that she used. Much of the Navy's food was tinned or salt-preserved and, in common with the rest of the country, rationing would determine the menu.

Our Instructor introduced himself to us. The three long service stripes and crossed-hook emblem sewed to the sleeves of his uniform denoted him to be a petty officer with at least twelve years of service. Later we found out he had served in the last war, completed his twenty-two years, and had been retained because of this war. He said in a loud voice "As a petty officer with my service I am next to god... don't ever forget that. When I ask you if you understand, you will answer Yes P.O!" Then he bellowed "Do you understand that" we all timidly answered "Yes P.O." to which he shouted, "Louder!" and this time in concert, we all shouted "Yes P.O!"

He now had our attention. In four weeks he would teach us the basics of parade drill, how to march as an orderly squad, how we would maintain and wear the mountain of kit we were issued, the way to mark and sew our names into every item and how to keep ourselves, as well as our bed space and dormitory, spotless and shipshape. What he taught us I am sure not one of us has forgotten. The next days would be spent drawing kit, not measured or fitted except by the experienced eye of the storekeeper, apart from the hats. We would have medical checks, injections and dental inspections. Harried from pillar to post we did everything on the double. After four weeks in nozzers we were ready to be allocated to a dorm in one of the divisions, and become members of a training class.

I could fill a book with idiosyncrasies of naval training and some already have. The navy was the only one of the services to take boys at age fifteen to train them, before posting them to what could be war situations, at age sixteen.

The advent of war attracted larger intakes of boys, and later on 'hostilities only' ratings (or HO's) as they were known. They had a shorter training course after having been called-up for service. Because these were men aged seventeen and over, they were kept separate from the boys who now numbered around two thousand. We knew very little of events outside of our confined world, or of the war's progress. We were kept busy from reveille, the morning bugle call at 06.30 hrs. Hearing this raucous call we would scramble from our bunk which had a horsehair mattress and itchy wool blankets. These then had to be then folded in a set manner and size, and our bed space left clean. Thirty boys would vie for space in the washroom, which was at the far end of the dorm and close to the heads (the naval term for toilets) whose stone floor felt very cold to stand on as we washed ourselves in icy water. The winter of 1939 was particularly harsh especially on the east coast, and it usually didn't suit the clothes we needed to wear for whichever activity we would be doing that morning. After morning parade and inspection, classes would double off to those activities. This would be seamanship and gunnery instruction mainly, but was sometimes interspersed with climbing the 180 ft. mast, a terror in itself, but especially so on a frosty or a windy day. We learnt to drill with rifles and to hone our marksmanship on the ranges. Our fitness increased, due to the time we spent rope-climbing or exercising on gym's wall-bars, or by playing sports out on the field, and also with boat pulling, and by sailing the heavy cutters and whalers out on the often icy and windswept River Orwell. Two weekday evenings there would be further schooling; including maths, English and naval history.

I was amazed that no person with any authority, from the recruiting officer onwards, seemed interested that I was trained as a motor mechanic and had leanings to the area of naval life where there was a demand for those skills. The opinion of a boy seaman would not be sought.

The only thing most of us boys had in common was probably our age and the fact that we were volunteers. Some had been cadets or scouts, and knew the basics of drill and smartness. A few like me were country boys, having easy going attitude and used to the great outdoors and with being alone with nature, while foraging in the woods and along the waysides. Others were from London, from Birmingham and from other cities of northern England. Many were streetwise and used to elbowing their way in, to make the best of any situation. They acted harder, but often I found this to be a veneer, armour they used as protection, because inside most were as timid as me. Never before had I heard such varied accents – 'scousers' from Liverpool, 'geordies' from the Tyneside, 'brummies' from Birmingham, the Scots and the Ulstermen, also those London 'cockneys' who would mimic country boys like me, and those others from Norfolk, Suffolk or wherever. Our class was typical; a melting pot, which had to be boiled down and moulded, to form the 'hearts of oak' that the Navy needed, to be smart, disciplined and ready to react to orders with little question. Many things we had to do, I and many others thought pointless, such as hauling a field gun around for instance.

Unfortunately for the population of the east coast and us at Ganges, with the German advance westward their towns and cities became a target for the Luftwaffe, and a threat to us. This brought a welcome respite and change for us. In May of 1940, six hundred Ganges boys were relocated to the Isle-of-Man, close to its capital Douglas. This entailed a move by train for us, complete with all our kit. We were packed in like cattle but we were in high spirits to be in the great outside. The remaining Ganges boys would leave the next day by train and head for other camps at Devonport or Liverpool.

The Living Years

After a long and circuitous rail journey we arrived at Fleetwood to catch the Manx Steam Packet which would ferry us to the port at Douglas on the Isle-of-Man, which is mid-way to Ireland in the Irish Sea. This would be my first voyage aboard a ship of any type.

On the train I had managed to get a window seat to watch the countryside unfold as we flashed by. The villages and towns seemed normal and at peace except that pill boxes and other defensive obstacles were being constructed to slow any enemy advance if the expected German invasion happened. The road signs and station names had been removed so it was difficult for me to know where we were. I got tired from gazing out at the moving images. With the rocking motion of the train, the effects of heat and fug created by a dozen boys in itchy serge uniforms, cramped in the compartment with cases and gasmasks (our kit bags and hammocks were stowed in the guard's van) I soon succumbed to join those already asleep and snoring.

Our destination was HMS St. George, a requisitioned holiday camp about a mile from Douglas. It had two separate areas connected by a tunnel under the road. Our billets were chalets, ten feet square, each housed four of us. The dining hall was a short distance from our chalet, there, each class was allocated two long tables. Being isolated in the Irish Sea, it was an ideal place to house prisoners of war and to have internment camps for civilians of enemy countries. What better place to inter boy seamen than behind barbed wire. I never quite understood this, we being patriotic volunteers, eager to go and fight. I don't think it was to stop anyone from breaking in, as outside was far more amenable. It was to prevent us from venturing out, even though we had no money to spend. I would, however, have loved to explore the surrounding countryside and the mountains further inland, but was never given the chance.

Here at St George, things seemed more relaxed, although the routine was much the same as before but without the mast to climb. The Instructors seemed more human, perhaps it was because we as a class had become more proficient and sure of ourselves. I began to excel at seamanship and boat-work which compensated for my lack of prowess in gunnery. I had become less timid and was able to hold my ground with the bigger, more forceful boys, even during the boxing bouts that were forced on us. The months soon passed and we knew that in November we would pass-out and be given our postings to a ship or an establishment, and then go home on Christmas leave.

Somewhere on the camp was a wireless set, and we got to hear snippets of news about the war, although much was censored. We did learn that Churchill had become prime minister at about the same time as our move to here. One instructor referred to him as an old drunk, another said that Churchill was a man of action and a champion of the navy. We had gathered around the wireless set to hear a recording of his first speech as Prime Minister to the House of Commons, 13th of May 1940, 'having nothing to offer but blood, toil, tears and sweat'. We thought then that we boys were giving all of those things on a daily basis. When he also said 'Come, let us go forward together', I didn't know then that in less than a year, I would be seeing him 'up close and personal' for many days.

With our relatively more relaxed routine I had more time to think of home and conjecture how mum was faring. Shortly before I left to join Ganges my mother had broken an ankle while shopping in Gloucester, after having slipped on a metal grating an access point for a cellar below street level.

Fortunately, she was able stay at the home of a relative until it mended, but I have always felt some guilt that I didn't stay home to care for her. The instructors always pressured us to write letters home, but knowing they censored what was written, I, like most other boys, would not put anything tender or sentimental in the letter. I would think of dad and wished I could have expressed my feelings to him while he was alive, but he went suddenly when I was very young. The lyrics of the song, 'The living years', which I would hear many years after that sad event sum up my feelings as well as any words I can say -

I know that I'm a prisoner

To all my Father held so dear

I know that I'm a hostage to all his hopes and fears

I just wish that I could have told him, in the living years

(Mike and The Mechanics released 1988)

Oggie Yafflers

The usual practice of 'their lordships', the term we gave to those at the Admiralty who decided our fate, was that a man's port division would be that from which it was easiest for him to travel home when going on any leave. My home port was to be Devonport. Any ship I would serve aboard would usually be one that was attached to that base when it was in home waters - but, as I was to find out, wartime requirement often precluded this. We, at Devonport, were known by those from other home ports as guzz ratings, or janners, and sometimes more disparagingly as oggie yafflers, but we took it as a term of honour because we felt superior to those 'pusser' pompey ships from Portsmouth or those chatty Chatham ratings with their up and at 'em Chatham attitude. Great rivalry existed between the three divisions which only evaporated when we clubbed together against the 'yanks', as we termed our American friends and allies.

From St George, we split up as a class, saying farewell to those heading to other ports, and also to our instructors, who had been our enemy in common, but who now were friendly as they wished us well, knowing that they would be judged by our future performance. Six of us headed south to Plymouth and more specifically to RN Barracks, Devonport.

On arrival we found the barracks to be full; men of all ranks and branches of the service, many had already been formed up into crews, ready to man the many ships, mainly destroyers but also frigates and corvettes, which were being launched from the shipyards. We were taken to the Crown Hill area of Plymouth; there we would be billeted in a tented camp erected as an overflow to the barracks. As soon as we had completed our joining routine we could take two weeks leave, so it wasn't long before I headed back northwards to Bulley. It seemed that I had joined the Navy to ride on trains.

Mum was as overjoyed to see me as I was to see her. She was full of questions and I think she was proud and worried in equal measure. It was nice to don civilian attire, but the clothes that I had parcelled up and sent home on my arrival at Ganges hardly fitted me now. During that year I had filled out with muscle and sinew although my height was much the same. Bulley and Huntley, although unchanged, were too quiet for me now after the hustle and bustle of frantic naval routine. I found it hard to relate to those boys of my age whose lives had been untouched by events in the wider world.

Many of those over eighteen had been conscripted or had volunteered for one of the armed forces. The older men would ask me questions, or give me their opinion on how things should be done. I was quite happy, at the end of the leave, to return to Crown Hill. There I waited some more, and fretted. Later, experience taught me that war was about training, preparation, anticipation and waiting. Action often came unexpectedly – frightening and frantic. It was then that training kicked in and proved its value. It was early February when the six of us received our posting - not to one of the workhorse escort vessels but to a mighty battleship... the brand spanking new, HMS Prince of Wales.

The Prince

Gazing in awe at the massive bulk of this floating arsenal, which looked impregnable, I wouldn't have believed that the days of these great battleships would soon be over. If I had known that within ten months, she would be smashed and broken, lying upside down in 230 feet of water, and that so many of these men who were busy about her decks and lofty upper-works would be gone with her, would I have felt as keen and excited as I was at that moment?... .I doubt it!

The Prince of Wales (we would refer to her as the Prince) was being readied for sea and all was hustle and bustle. I didn't know then that she had already been the subject of a Luftwaffe attack during August and had suffered extensive damage, which was now repaired. Stores were being loaded aboard; a back-breaking task that tomorrow we would be involved in. First we had to get our kit aboard and do a joining routine.

142 boy seamen were part of the ship's company which numbered about 1,600 men. Our mess was forward, two decks below the upper deck. We would sleep in hammocks which had to be rigged above the scrubbed wooden mess tables and stowed away during the day. Each mess had an Instructor, and as usual boys were kept separate from the men and had their own duties to perform. My work station, when not on watch, would be right aft on the quarterdeck, about as far as it was possible to be from my mess. My action station was on P4, a 5.25" gun mounting, sited aft on the port side of the ship at upper deck level; I worked below the turret in the cordite handling room, other boys would be in the shell handling room adjacent. These two areas, being an integral part of the whole mounting revolved with the turret when it was trained around in either direction. The Prince had eight of these turrets each with twin guns. These were anti-aircraft guns, as were the 32 Pom-Pom guns, (the name derived from the sound they made when firing) which were in quadruple mountings. The main, heavy armament, were the ten 14-inch guns, which were housed in three turrets, two forward and one aft. I worked in the shadow of this after-turret when at my work station.

About a week later, after we had stored the ship, we moved down-river to enable us to take on-board ammunition and cordite for stowage in the cooled magazines, which were sited

below the gun mountings. It was back-breaking work, humping boxes of ammunition of all types.

We lived like rabbits in a warren; the ship a labyrinth; hundreds of watertight compartments, through which we needed to scoot, as woe betide any who failed to be at their action station by becoming trapped in one of the compartments when doors were shut and clipped. There were armoured hatches between decks, with vertical steel ladders going down, on other hatches, ladders were angled; like that which we had to descend en-route to our mess-deck, while trying to balance against the roll and pitch of the ship, when carrying food-filled mess trays that we had collected from the central galley.

 Our orders, by voice, bugle or by the boatswain's call, were announced over the raucous loud-speaker system.

Although the ship was not yet ready and fit for war (because there were problems with the main armament, and those problems were still being worked on), we sailed to Scapa Flow, where we would 'work up' the new ship, and us the crew, would train to be action ready.

The Battle of the Denmark Strait

At and around Scapa Flow, throughout April and May we practised and trained. The ships engines were tested and proved. Anti-aircraft guns, including our turret, were tested and the gun-crew performance honed as we fired at targets towed by aircraft. We were being readied for something 'their lordships' thought might be in the offing. We were at Scapa, not just for our safety, because all three of the home ports and their surrounds would be heavily bombed by the Germans, but also because it was closer to the expected action.

Intelligence had reported that the battleship Bismarck together with the cruiser Prinz Eugen had departed their protected berth in the Norwegian Fiords. The Home Fleet, under Admiral Tovey who was in our sister ship King George V, deployed to the North Atlantic around Iceland on the 22nd May to be ready to intercept Bismarck, at whatever route she chose to take.

The Bismarck was newly built and was more than capable of out-performing any one of our ships. By ignoring the naval treaties which the British had adhered to, designed to limit the size and power of battleships, they had built the Bismarck and Tirpitz - both mammoths.

The Prince, together with our leader Hood and six destroyers, would take up position to the south of Iceland. The route Bismarck chose to take was through the Denmark Straits, close to the Arctic pack ice, so this put us in prime position to attack her first and allow the remainder of the Fleet to catch up and home in for the kill.

What did I know of these happenings at the time? Precious little. We spent many hours closed up at our action stations. So many that we needed to be fed. Sandwiches and tea would be taken round to all stations.

It was now the 24th May. Below decks, shut in our isolated steel compartment, again we waited not knowing if or when our turret would be called into action. It turned out that we never were, as no aircraft were involved in action against us. The first we knew of the sighting of Bismarck was when our big guns opened fire. We would hear the thunder and crash of our main armament and could feel the massive shudder and hear the tremendous bangs, as shells from Bismarck and Prinz Eugen struck the Prince. It wasn't until hours later we were told that one shell from Bismarck had destroyed much of our bridge as it passed through without exploding. Only the Captain and Chief Yeoman survived this event, the rest of the bridge crew were killed. Apparently, we had taken four hits from Bismarck and three from Prinz Eugen, two, being below the water line caused major flooding. Another shell, which fortunately failed to detonate, struck and was lodged just below my action station. My guardian angel seemed to be at work again.

Amongst these happenings I felt a massive tremor, after which the small hatch above my head opened, and one of the turret crew-members peered down and shouted "Hood's gone", then he slammed the hatch shut again. We looked at each other in puzzlement wondering what he meant by GONE. It wasn't until after this phase of the battle had ended that we found out the awful truth. Only three survived from Hood's crew which numbered 1418 men. There are many theories to explain the possible cause of the massive explosion which I won't go into here. Suffice to say, Hood was due extensive modifications which were cancelled due to the war. Apparently, our ship had turned away just in time to avoid her wreckage.

Throughout this action our main armament turrets, not working properly, were unable to fire full salvos. If they had been we might have damaged Bismarck more. The three hits we scored on Bismarck resulted in her shipping an estimated 2,000 tons of water forward, putting one of her generators out of action and ripping open fuel tanks. Bismarck was now listing to port and leaking fuel oil, leaving a trail to be followed, and that fuel loss would limit her range. Luckily the German Admiral had overruled Bismarck's Captain, who wanted to follow and destroy us.

You may wonder how we spent our time at 'action stations' while waiting for action that didn't always happen. I was rooted to my particular station, as was my opposite number (or oppo in naval parlance). It was we two who had to provide the cordite charge to the two guns. I served the left gun whereas my oppo served that on the right. Opposite was a good description for the two of us; I, being small and beautifully formed, struggled to reach up to place the charge into what was called the cordite-ring. My oppo, boy seaman Owen (we called him Wilfred, after the poet) was 6 feet tall, and built like a barn door; he could hold the charge in one hand and effortlessly place it up.

You must bear in mind that we were in competition, one gun against the other, and our turret's crew against the others. As you know the strength of any chain is the strength of its weakest link, and I didn't want to be the cause of any breakage in our particular chain. I feared the 'powers that be' in our gunnery world, more than I feared the enemy.

Wilf also had trained at Ganges, two classes ahead of me. He loved Ganges saying it was a great improvement on his home, a Glasgow tenement, a 'back to back', as he called it. At least that's what I think he said (having met a couple of parrots and a Minor Bird I could understand better than I could Wilf), anyway while we were waiting, which was often, he loved to hear about how I lived out in the countryside; about mum's food, how I caught rabbits, about the Severn bore - everything and anything. He never tired of it, saying that when this war is over he was going to come to live at Bulley.

When we were told the fate of Hood, he mentioned that boys from his Ganges class had been full of excitement at being posted to her. You can imagine the joy, and his in particular, when on the 27th May, news arrived that Bismarck had been sunk by ships and aircraft of our Fleet. An eye for an eye, as the saying goes.

> *Lend him to stroke these blind bullet-leads,*
>
> *which, long to nuzzle in the heart of lads,*
>
> *or, give him cartridges of fine zinc teeth*
>
> *sharp, with the sharpness of grief and death*
>
> **Wilfred Owen**

"At long last, Mr President" – Winston S Churchill. "Glad to have you aboard. Mr Churchill" – Franklin Delano Roosevelt.

Now in fighting trim our repairs completed we were at sea with our speeding bow pointing to the west, towards Newfoundland, which was then a British colony. Why Newfoundland? Well it was because, symbolically, it was half-way between London and Washington. Our secret mission was to convey one of the two most powerful war-time leaders to meet the other – the first time they would meet face to face. Newfoundland was neutral ground. We had Winston Churchill on board, on his way to meet the US President, Roosevelt. As he had climbed our gangway with a cigar clamped in his teeth, he raised his hand to give his trademark 'V for victory' sign, our officers saluted him and the crew cheered him aboard.

The ship headed into Atlantic rollers, foaming green water breaking over our bow, which would bury itself as far back as 'A' turret, before breaking itself free and rising again to meet the next oncoming roller. Spray would fly aft to where I was, peering through my binoculars as I scanned a sector of the horizon and sky, while carrying out my duty as one of the bridge lookouts. We knew that U-boats would be out searching for targets, either merchant convoys, or ships such as the Prince. Long range German aircraft could attack at any moment. Woe-betide the lookout not sharp enough to sight a threat before one of the watch officers did. My sector was from dead ahead to 15 degrees to port, which is why I could see the bow. I had to resist the desire to duck when the curtain of spray hurtled towards me. Trying to keep my binoculars on the horizon to spot the merest whisper of funnel smoke, or the truck of a ships mast which was below the horizon, was an art, but, as a country boy able to spot a skylark in the cow pasture or the ears of a hare, crouched low in the hayfield, I considered myself an expert. I felt at home and by now I was used to the motion of the ship, but alas, too often I was carrying out the more mundane tasks that we boys had to suffer. Before breakfast each day, along with other boy seamen, about ten of us, with trousers rolled up to the knee, we scrubbed the wood-boarding of the quarterdeck using our long-handled scrubbers. After breakfast I would be employed in that general area but had to keep clear when senior officers 'took the air' on deck. Some mornings I would see Mr. Churchill, pacing to and fro. He would wear some kind of boiler suit, and he seemed comfortable to be at sea, but seemed to have much on his mind.

Sheltering in the lee of the huge Y turret, the after main armament, I often chatted with a wardroom steward. He was an H.O. rating, a native of London. According to him he was educated at Dulwich College, until being conscripted. He told me Churchill was worried because FDR (Roosevelt) was a poker-player, and he held all the cards. Churchill, he said, played chess. Our British Empire that he was hoping to protect was his king. (In my naivety then, I thought his words far-fetched, but with events since the war's end, I think he was right). He did also enlighten me that nations didn't have friends only interests, whatever the two leader's personal rapport might be. One morning the steward advised me to keep the cigar stub-ends I had collected from where Churchill had tossed them. He said each would be worth a week's pay to me, later in life. I kept them in my locker, stored in an empty cigar tin the steward had given me, together with the gift–box that sailors of USS Augusta had presented us with when we met.

On the 9th August we entered the sheltered anchorage of Placentia Bay, Newfoundland, and moored close to the heavy cruiser USS Augusta which had FDR aboard. The American people thought he was on a ten-day fishing trip. We would remain there until the 14th August, which allowed three days for the meetings between the two leaders. As a result of these meetings, the Atlantic Charter was drawn-up; this defined the allied nations wartime goals and became a basis for post-war order. On the Sunday, a church service was conducted on our quarterdeck. Many officers and some men from both ships attended, along with the two leaders. Seating for the service was informal, men from both Navies intermingled. The specially chosen hymns 'O God our help in ages past' and 'Onward Christian Soldiers' followed by the Navy anthem 'For those in peril on the sea' in full and hearty voice, I doubt such a scene could be replicated aboard a ship of Nazi Germany or its Fascist satellite Italy.

Returning home with Churchill aboard, one day we steamed between the lines of ships which formed a massive merchant convoy, bound for the US. The crews of these ships seemed to know that Churchill was aboard us, because each passing ship sounded her siren, and their crews waved and cheered, responding to Churchill's V sign. Whatever else he might have been, he was a figure of hope for all, and his rousing speeches spurred us on. As I watched those ships of many nationalities, some old and struggling to keep up with the convoy and all having few defensive weapons – sitting ducks you might say – I felt great admiration for the merchant seamen that crewed them.

'Fancy twice a knight at your age.'

To - Admiral, Sir James Sommerville (already knighted), on receiving his second knighthood to reward his successful handling of force H.

From – Admiral, of the Fleet, Sir Andrew B. Cunningham.

We would not grow any barnacles at Scapa, within a month we were heading south to cross the Bay of Biscay en-route for Gibraltar and the Mediterranean Sea, along with two other battleships, five cruisers and eighteen destroyers, with air cover provided by an aircraft carrier. We were known as force H; twenty-seven ships of war, to ensure that nine, fast merchant ships, heavily laden with vital food supplies and war materials, would reach the beleaguered island of Malta, the base from which our armed forces could try to halt the axis advance in North Africa.

Passing Gibraltar on the 24th September, we were then vulnerable to attack by Italian ships and aircraft. We constantly practiced closing-up to our action stations and bringing the guns to a state of readiness. It was during one of these events that an awful accident occurred, the memory of which haunts me to this day. The gun-crews would usually man the turret via the upper deck, because that was where it was situated, while those boys, who like me worked in the shell or cordite handling rooms, would man their station through the deck below. On this occasion one man of the turret's crew had come through from the deck below. I was about to duck down under what is known as the shell-ring to man my station, but, this man who needed to get up into the turret, tapped me on my shoulder and said "Let me go first and I'll be out of your way." That made sense, as once I had manned my position there was hardly space for another to get through. I moved back; he ducked under the ring, and as he did so the turret was trained around, it trapped the man and cut his body in half at waist level. I will not try to describe his horrific screams or the words that he tried to mouth, but the memory of them has caused me nightmares ever since. This should not be described as inadvertent, it was pure stupidity on the part of the captain of the turret, and against gunnery procedure, which states that the turret should not be trained until the crew are at their positions. I was never called to give any statement about this incident and have no idea of its outcome, but I have always wondered how this was described to the man's next of kin. Maybe it was put down as 'killed in action'. What I do realise is that it would have been me, if things had been different.

Three days later, the heaviest of the expected air attacks occurred. As usual, Wilf and I had been waiting. Dressed in our overalls and also the white, fire resistant anti-flash hoods which covered most of our face and shoulders and wearing gloves which came almost to the elbow – we were sweating. I said to Wilf that it reminded me of the heat of the milking parlour; twenty cows impatient to be milked, steam arising from their smelly excrement as I awaited my turn to get milk, along with the others, also clutching their pails. The milking

was being done by the old-fashioned hand method, so it was a slow process. Wilf would get his milk from the doorstep, delivered by the milkman in a bottle, he said.

Air attacks are usually very sudden, giving the attackers an advantage. The gun-crews, their sharpness blunted by fatigue and lulled by in-action, have to react to aircraft diving out of the sun, then, possibly changing aim to counter threats from other directions. Once any action started, we lost all track of time. It was fast and furious, the cacophony of sound reverberating in our steel chamber was deafening from the continuous firing from our turret, which ravenously consumed the cordite we fed it with. We would earn no medals or knighthoods, but we did prove ourselves not to be the weakest link. It was reward enough for me when Wilf put his big, brawny arm around my shoulders, and said "Ye are a braw, wee Sassenach, CJ". At least, that's what I think he said!

The battleship, Nelson, was damaged by a torpedo. In retribution, our guns blazed away and we either shot down, or badly damaged the aircraft that delivered it. In total eight Italian aircraft were lost to our Fleet's combined barrage. Unfortunately, between Rodney and ourselves, we shot down two Fairey Fulmars, from the aircraft carrier Ark Royal. So-called, 'friendly fire'. The merchant convoy reached harbour intact and Malta lived to fight another day.

Unsinkable British battleship

There was an atmosphere of excitement in the boy's mess when we were told that our next voyage was to the Far East. It was probably not so for the married men in the crew, as it would mean a long separation from their wives and children, whom they saw little of even though we were in the Home Fleet. Our destination, in fact, was Singapore, an exotic place that was the subject of many yarns told by some of the 'Jack-Tars' on our ship. Our first port of call was Cape Town, or more specifically, at the naval base at Simonstown, close by. There was to be no secrecy this time, the Cape Argus newspaper heralded the arrival of 'unsinkable British battleship, on her way to Singapore'. We had arrived together with other ships, including the old aircraft carrier, Hermes.

The newer carrier Indomitable should have been with us to provide air-cover, but had run aground at Kingston, Jamaica and had gone to the US for repair.

The bright lights and the girls of Cape Town provided distraction for us boys, away from our hum-drum existence aboard the ship. Many crew-members, including me, were sorry when it was time to continue our voyage. The Hermes did not sail with us, as she was considered too slow. Our next port of call was the Indian Ocean island of Mauritius. This proved to be an equally exciting place for a country boy like me, as it was for others. Many of these boys had been raised in deprived circumstances, yet here, among the happy, light-hearted Mauritian girls, we were treated as if we were princes. With them, we could dance and sing, and have fun. With hindsight, for some of these boys, and for many others of our crew, it would prove to be the last such frivolity they would ever enjoy.

Flying fish were skimming from our bow-wave as we headed across the calm ocean to the Maldives. Our destination was Addu Atoll, a place which provided a calm, safe anchorage at all times, because of the barrier reefs of coral shielding it from the storms. At the anchorage we were amongst dolphins, and sometimes whales would break surface alongside the ship, it seemed we had arrived in paradise. The atoll was fringed by white sandy beaches and flanked with coconut palms. We only stayed for two days, and on the second of those days our ship provided early Christmas dinner, with attendant festive trimmings, for the Royal Marine detachment that was based there to provide protection for Gan Airfield. This important military airfield was built on one of the nearby islands and was used by the RAF throughout the war. I spent the little free time that I had, swimming off one of the Atoll's beaches, not realising that the next time I would swim would be in horrific circumstances, just a few weeks later.

Arriving at Singapore, there was tension in the air due to Japan's territorial expansion. We had to prepare for confrontation with them, and as usual we trained, and waited. We didn't have long to wait; we were at action stations very early on the 8th December, our anti-aircraft armament, including the guns of our turret, were soon in action against a swarm of Japanese bombers. Our intense barrage probably thwarted their attack, as none of our ships were damaged.

There have been many an 'if', 'but' or 'may-be' since then, regarding the situation in the Far East, about the defences of Singapore itself, or what would have happened if we did have the air-cover we needed. The reality of the situation was that we sailed without air-cover in company with the battle-cruiser Repulse. We would endeavour to disrupt the Japanese landings, by confronting them in the South China Sea.

Death of a Prince

After we had left Singapore we spent a lot of our time at action stations. Our objective, it seems, was to intercept the Japanese invasion fleet north of Malaya but we had failed in that objective and were returning to Singapore when we were attacked while in open waters by long-range torpedo bombers. I knew nothing of our Admiral's intentions or any of these events while at my action station. Once our ship's AA guns opened fire Wilf and I were busy supplying the cordite needed to maintain the heavy rate of gun-fire.

Here isolated below, as we were, not able to communicate with each other due to the ear-defenders which we wore to protect our eardrums, we were aware that our turret's two guns had stopped firing, because they stopped consuming cordite, and the noise abated. During any action, our brains would have to compute and make sense of the various noises and explosions we heard. We could normally tell which ones were either a near-miss, or a hit on our ship from the jolt which they imparted, and the shudder that went throughout the ship resulting from a bomb or torpedo detonation. Not an easy after-effect to describe in a few words. We removed the ear-plugs and it was only then that we became aware of silence, the hum of electrical power had stopped. This usual ever-present background noise was gone, the noise which our brain would ignore until it was no longer there. Our guns had stopped firing, possibly that was due to the lack of electrical power, but also at this time the ship had developed a list to port and those guns on our side of the ship could not elevate enough to fire at even low flying attackers, and many guns sited on the starboard side would not be able to depress down enough to fire at them either. Wilf and I looked at each other in wonder as the list kept increasing. We had had no communication from the turret above, therefore I pushed up on the small hatch, which was above my head and led into the turret. I did not expect it to open, as usually one of the gun crew would be standing on it. The hatch opened easily, I looked into the turret and was amazed to find it empty, both of the gun crews had gone. I shouted down to Wilf, and to those others "They've gone – let's scarper". I made my way up, went through the turret and out onto the deck and Wilf followed behind me. I don't know what the others did, but as we all usually manned our stations through the decks below, I guessed that was the way they chose to exit. Subsequently, I read accounts detailing the route they would have taken which led through the cinema flat. That was where a bomb, which after penetrating through from the upper deck, had then exploded, creating a cavernous void. That area was where many of our wounded had been gathered, and I have no doubt that is where they, and those six boys of our ammunition supply-chain, met their end.

I lost sight of Wilf, and I thought perhaps he had gone forward to where a destroyer was alongside, taking off those of our crew who were not at an essential action station. Going aft to the quarterdeck looked a clearer route to me, because I could see obstacles as I looked forward. I was working on instinct; my brain trying to rationalise the situation and to work out my best course of action. I could see that the sea around us was littered with floating debris, amongst which bodies were floating. I had heard no call to abandon ship but could see that with the ship almost on her side and with water lapping half-way across the quarterdeck, that wood-planked area where Churchill had paced and where he and Roosevelt had met our officers did not symbolize status now, no more a place for pomp and ceremony it looked forlorn and uninviting so I reasoned that the sensible thing to do was to leave the ship. I removed my boots, tied the laces together, and placed them under a fan-trunk ... for safety! Perhaps I was thinking that if the ship did not sink and could somehow be saved, I would then be able to retrieve the boots; or was this action a result of the intense indoctrination us boys suffered. With the sea lapping at my feet I merely had to release my handhold and walk into the water. My aim was to get clear of the ship, and away from the towering super-structure and also the gun turret, now leaning over and above me at an alarming angle. Fearing the ship would soon roll over, I wanted to be clear of any suction or disturbances that may cause. Fortunately, with the sea being calm I could swim easily, but in my brain I had a mixture of hopes and fears: hope that I could find a suitable piece of floating debris, or a rescuer: fear of ingesting oil, which was now spreading across the calm surface, and the fear of sharks. We would see sharks, those lean mean killing machines, gathering around our waste-food chute when we were in harbour, so I knew they abounded in these waters. I seemed to be alone on a wide, wide, sea and I came to realise why we had trained at Ganges to be able to swim wearing overalls, the very clothing that we had to wear when at action-stations.

When your face is just above surface level you have limited field of vision, therefore you can imagine my relief when a Carley float came into my view. I am not sure of the distance, but after I had swum for about twenty minutes I was able to grab a rope-loop attached to its side. These loops were fitted for this purpose, to be used when the float is fully occupied, as this one was. Carley floats come in various sizes; this one was designed to seat a dozen men and It was already overfull, with no room for me. I held on tight trying to keep my head above water and my legs as high up as possible and all the time I worried about sharks.

Why he chose to do it I don't know, but one of these men on the float suddenly stood up and shouted "I'm going back to the ship"; someone else tried to persuade him not to go, but others, fearing that his wild attitude was a threat to the stability of the float, said "No, let him go if he wants to", and with that the man jumped off the float into the water, and swam in the direction of the ship. I don't know his fate and can only hope he was saved from the sea, but I do know he never made it back to the ship, for within a few minutes of his leaving, the Prince rolled over and gradually sank below the surface. His leaving probably saved my life, or at the very least, my legs from the sharks, because I was then able to take his place on the raft.

How many hours we spent jammed together on the raft I don't know as I had no means of telling the time. Who those other men were, and what had been their method of escape I never discovered. Each individual's own experience was probably different from that of any other.

There were many acts of bravery that day because I do know that those few guns that were able to, were still firing almost until the end. At times, aircraft were overhead trying to locate survivors. One flew low, crossing above our position, we waved, cheered, and gave a 'thumbs-up' signal. We saw a destroyer, which turned out to be the Express; she some distance away and was either searching for, or picking up other survivors. Gradually she made her way in our direction, and I think it was early evening when she took us aboard. Her decks were already crammed with other survivors of our ship, some of them in pitiful condition. When I clambered aboard her my bare feet burnt on contact with her iron decks, but fortunately I managed to clamber up and sit astride some mine-sweeping equipment which was on her deck. I later discovered that Express had remained alongside the Prince until the last possible moment, she cast off and went astern as the ship was in her final death-throes.

I am the only living survivor

.

The Prince settled by the head and slowly sank below the surface taking with her those unable to make their escape, and also the Captain and the Admiral who it seems had chosen to remain with the ship.

This whole disastrous episode was played out in about one hour; from when our guns began to fire until I boarded the raft. The longest hour I have ever spent, and also the most horrific. I had watched as men tried desperately to climb down from superstructure on the ship, others trying to swim through thick floating oil, and some who were so close to the ship, they wouldn't survive the suction caused by her sinking. Down with my ship went everything I possessed, except for the pair of wet overalls in which I was now clad. Gone also, was my box containing cigar stubs, and the gift-box I had received from crew-members of USS Augusta. Far more important to me, Wilf, and those other six boys from our action-stations were also gone. That fateful day, we lost 327 of our crew, along with another 513, who were lost from Repulse. I had served aboard Prince the length of her commission, but knew few of them by sight, and even fewer by name.

Subsequent to the war, a survivor's association was formed. Over the following years I heard many individuals own account of that day, and I formed many lasting friendships. Time has taken its toll on that membership, until today when as far as I know I am the only surviving member of those who actually served on the ship. There are a number of associate members; those who were the spouses, or other family members of the survivors. Considering I was only 17 at the time of the sinking, and one of the youngest of the crew, I suppose my being the last survivor is a fair result. I did learn from a fellow member, that the captain of the turret (he who should have made sure we got out from our stations) was found guilty at court martial. I do not know what punishment he was awarded, all I do know is that I was never called to witness against him; I had however included the facts in the statement I had given, back in 1941.

No Ice-cream today

The survivors of both ships, numbering over 2000 men, were taken back to Singapore and housed in what was known as fleet shore accommodation. I was billeted in one of the tents used to supplement the camp. We became just another part of what seemed general chaos, among a disparate group of people. Not only us the survivors of sunken ships, but others, both military and civilians who had arrived from outlying places which were about to be overrun by the Japanese advance. During this period, all survivors were asked to give a 'statement of fact' ; an account of what happened in their area of the ship, a jigsaw of events, to be pieced together with time, to enable an overall picture to emerge.

The local lordships were trying to create order from the chaos. Sometimes a loudspeaker message would call for certain persons, to report somewhere, to an office perhaps. These persons probably had some specialisation, or skill, required for a particular purpose. One day, a message blared out, "Boy Seaman C. Peacey, report immediately to the jetty". The message was repeated: the normal manner for any announcement to be made. This message came at an inconvenient time for me. It came as I was nearing the front of a long queue, which I had been in for about twenty minutes. The reason for the queue was an issue of ice-cream, a very rare and welcome treat. I was faced with a dilemma; should I comply immediately, or should I wait until I got my ice-cream. The decision that I made probably saved me from a number of years internment by the Japanese, and from all the horror that would have entailed. Perhaps they would have sent me to work on the infamous Burma-Siam railway. The announcement, and my compliance to the demand, may well have saved my life because a couple of weeks after then, on the 16th of February, Singapore itself was taken by the Japanese.

I got to the jetty and was directed to board the light cruiser Danae to replace one of her boy seamen, for some reason unknown to me at that time. Why it was Boy Seaman Peacey, of all the other boy seamen also in that camp, I will never know. The person who made that decision and the one who called out the announcement probably spent the remainder of their war in some form of internment, along with all those others, both in that queue and in the shore accommodation. The Danae, still with her engines turning-over, was waiting only long enough to pick up whatever things, or people, she had to embark – within ten minutes we were at sea.

The beautiful daughter of the King, of Argos

My joining of Danae was far from being by the traditional method. I merely crossed her gangplank and was directed to the quarterdeck. I only had the clothes I was wearing; tropical issue shorts and shirt. Items I was issued with on arrival at the shore accommodation. I did no joining routine I just reported to the killick of the quarterdeck work-party. (Any of those of leading rate are referred to in the Navy as being a killick, a term for an anchor, on account of the anchor emblem which is sewed to their uniform sleeve. To add to your confusion, the Navy nickname for any having the surname of Walker is hooky, which is also another slang title for those of leading rate. The nickname hooky is also derived from the anchor or 'hook' as it is often referred to). This leading seaman had the surname Walker. Any who have been in the Navy, will understand all of this Naval jargon which I have tried to avoid in the main, so the book is easily understandable for the layman to read.

At the quarter-deck, Hooky Walker was supervising the taking in, and the stowing, of the stern mooring ropes. He directed me to assist in doing this. The sea seemed to be boiling, the effect of our propellers between our stern and the jetty as we swung outwards. The head-rope being kept taut assisted in this manoeuvre, and before long when the head-rope was let go, the ship was facing in the opposite direction and soon was powering away, to leave Singapore behind. Hooky, in admiration, said to me "Our skipper could perform Swan Lake on a pinhead". In time, I found out that Hooky had similar skills, not in ship-handling but as coxswain of the Captain's motor boat – I will tell you more about that later.

I became a quarterdeck-man again, but here, I worked within a totally different environment to that aboard the regimented atmosphere of a battleship. Here it was friendly and relaxed. Danae, with any stretch of a vivid imagination you could not describe as she was described in Greek mythology, as being 'the beautiful daughter of the king, of Argos'. This old weather-beaten light cruiser of first war vintage had been on the Far East station for two years and was soon to return to the UK for refit. In the meantime, for the next three months she was attached to 'China force' in the Yellow Sea, and also between the Dutch East Indies (the present-day Indonesia) and Ceylon. We were part of a strike force led by the Dutch admiral Doorman, and was made up of American, British, Dutch and Australian ships. This small fleet sailed to intercept a similar sized force of Japanese ships somewhere in the Java Sea. Fate intervened once more, to 'save my bacon', as the saying goes. Danae and our sister ship Durban, were detached from the force and ordered to proceed to Colombo. Most other ships of that strike force were sunk by units of the Japanese fleet. Many lives were lost, including that of the admiral.

It turned out the reason for me joining Danae was that some members of her original complement of 15 boy seamen, had by now reached age 18, and became ordinary seamen in man's service, I replaced one of those.

You will be aware that at the same time Japan was attacking Singapore, they also, without warning, attacked the US base at Pearl Harbour, Hawaii, almost 8,000 miles from Singapore. That attack was on a Sunday morning, 7th December 1941. Two US battleships were sunk, and a further six were damaged. It was described by Roosevelt as 'a day that will live in infamy'. On the 8th December, the U.S declared war on Japan, and would no longer only be arming friendly nations to fight, but also be expanding her own armed forces massively. By the time I returned to the Far East in 1944, the US Pacific fleet was more powerful than the whole of the Royal Navy, and no longer would we rule the waves.

Hooky Walker said to me "Who but a fool would wake and provoke a sleeping tiger". An attack like this seemed to fly in the face of the Samurai code of honour, discipline and morality, which was supposedly the basic code of conduct for Japanese society. The same day as America did, the Dutch government in-exile, also declared war on Japan. It was for these reasons that the Danae now would be working together with US and Dutch ships, to protect the convoys.

A ship is known by her boats

Little of our time, on this ship, was wasted with 'spit and polish', or with scrubbing the wood planked quarter-deck. Hooky's interest lay with the motor boat, having recently become its coxswain. Its previous one was probably too staid for the likes of our swashbuckling captain. The motor-boat was as weather-beaten as our ship and needed sprucing up. Being what is known in the Navy as a 'dab-hand' with a paint brush, I was soon employed laying a gloss blue coat over the boat's faded paint-work. The boat's engine was as tired as was its paintwork and it had not been as reliable as Hooky, and more importantly, as the captain desired. Unfortunately, the Danae's own engines were tired also, demanding the full attention of the ship's engineers, so that they could produce the power and the speed our captain demanded of them.

I told Hooky that I was a qualified motor mechanic, conveniently omitting the word 'apprentice', and as such I had maintained similar petrol-fuelled engines to those fitted to this twin-screw, hard-chine, motor-boat, (its description in naval parlance). I checked the engine maintenance-plan which showed that the routine, 1,000 hour overhaul had not been carried out. I also found that the lubricating oil in the engine's sump was congealed. As any marine engineer will know, a boat's engines are called on to perform arduous duties, as they run nearly at full power when the boat is underway and are frequently required to develop high power with little or no warming up. The commissioned engineer, responsible for the ship's boats (as well as a host of other things) allowed me to carry out routine maintenance. He would check any adjustments that I made to the carburettors, or to the flow of circulating water, etc. I serviced the engine-controls and the steering gear, as well as the electric ignition system, also I ensured that the bilges were always as clean and petrol-vapour free, as they should be. I became part of the boat's crew, and this would be my main duty when the ship was in harbour. We would often be called on when our captain had to visit the captains of other ships of the escort. Naval lore states that, 'a ship is known by its boats' our motorboat now would run as fast and as efficiently as its makers had laid down, just the way our captain wanted it to.

I learned much from Hooky Walker about boat handling and boat operations. I didn't know then that seventeen years later this knowledge would stand me in good stead, when I became the boat coxswain for the distinguished Captain Morgan-Giles, DSO, OBE, GM., the captain of HMS Vernon, Portsmouth, (later he become Admiral, Sir Morgan-Giles, and later still, conservative member of parliament for Winchester).

My memories of those three months include the scent of the flora, the sounds of tropical birdsong, and the wild-animal calls of Ceylon of the Indonesian Islands, and of Sumatra.

We were escorting slow ships, of all types and of many nationalities. Sometimes, we fired our guns in anger at marauding Japanese aircraft and when we did parts of our ship would fly off, as did the galley door which one time that I just happened to be leaning on as our AA-guns opened fire. I think we caused more actual damage to ourselves than to those aircraft, but we did dissuade them from getting close enough to cause damage, either to us or to any of our flock.

On returning to the UK, I left Danae, just before she was taken to the Tyne for refit. Towards the end of the war this 'beautiful daughter of the King, of Argos', changed her name to Conrad when she was transferred to the Polish navy. She went on to serve them well.

Well, I woke up this morning, you were on my mind

Written by Sylvia Fricker in 1962 and sung by Crispian St. Peters. Those words are as true for me today, as they were in 1942.

I was entitled to survivors leave and had to take it before going back to guzz, to find out what next their lordships, or more correctly the drafting office at RN barracks, had in store for me. My surprise arrival at our home was a thrill for mum, and she made a great fuss of me. The local area was even quieter than before, many young men had left to join the services, their work on the farm being done by those older, or by 'land army' women.

My 'local', the Red Lion in Huntley only opened between 8pm and 10pm because beer was rationed due to wartime restrictions. The pub was always welcoming, which was probably the reason so many passers-by would break their road journey to take refreshment there. Inside the pub the dart-board was often in use, but by challenging the game's winner, I usually managed to get to the board. Once on, I rarely lost a game. I seemed to have a natural talent for darts even though I had little chance to practice. Listening to conversations while playing, I learned that Huntley had a new policeman, the previous one having retired. Constable Dobbs had been transferred from the police headquarters at Gloucester to take over the rural area of Huntley which he administered from the police house opposite the pub. By all accounts he was a fair man and not at all judgemental. They also said that he would often call into the pub, though he never drank more than a half pint of beer. However, it seemed that the main interest for the young men, and some of the not so young men, was that he had a very attractive daughter. She was just fourteen, they said, not that the fact seemed to worry them. What probably concerned them more was that she seemed to have no interest in the local beaux. Her interests were more academic, she was a prize-winning student of history, and of poetry, at the Newent grammar school she attended. This was a rare occurrence for anyone of this locality to go to any school other to the one in Huntley. This local chit-chat was of little interest to me, having seen countless attractive and perhaps more exotic girls in South Africa or Singapore, and at Indian Ocean islands between those two places.

The last Saturday evening of my leave, I was waiting outside the Red Lion for it to open, when a slender and shapely young woman came cycling past. She wore white shorts and a blue blouse which was loose over them, as she rode her fairish hair was ruffled by the breeze. She paid me not a glance as she pedalled past, seeming to be intent on the road ahead of her.

Just one look - that's all it took, and she was on my mind.

She would become the love of my life

I was posted to HMS Defiance, a torpedo-branch school, to be trained as a torpedo-man. This training took place aboard two old hulks, former 'men of war', ships of the Napoleonic war era. I had found my niche, having dreaded the thought of being a gunner. Torpedo handling and maintenance involve both mechanics and electrics, both of which hold my interest. When aboard a ship not fitted with torpedoes, the torpedo-men would form part of the ship's electrical team. While a ship itself is powered by whatever engines she has, virtually all equipment aboard is powered by electricity.

I passed the course with 'flying colours', as they say, and was sent back to barracks to join Naval Party 567. There were several of these 'parties', whose purpose would be revealed to us once we needed to know. In the mean-time any that had annual leave due to them were instructed to use it up. I, being one of those, soon found myself back home in Bulley enjoying another seven days leave.

In the Red Lion the evening conversations were usually quite boring for me, such as "Farmer Giles has got one of those new-fangled tractors" or "We got a heavy crop of turnips this year, out of the top field", etc, etc. It was during one of these exciting evenings that P.C. Dobbs called in the bar to have his half pint of beer. He came over to me and said "Mrs. Dobbs would like you to come visit us for supper on Saturday evening, and both of us would like to hear everything that has happened to you since you joined up".

It was a pleasant evening, Mr. and Mrs. Dobbs were good company and it was the start of something huge in my life. I was to find out, eventually, that this invite had been instigated by the young, very attractive Beryl Dobbs, even though during the course of that Saturday evening, she seemed to pay little attention to me. At that time Beryl was still at school studying history, her main interest, but was also practicing shorthand, before taking the various levels of examination. She left school at sixteen and was employed at the Shire Hall in Gloucester, home of the county council, where she worked until her father transferred to work in the Bristol area, a year later. I didn't realise then, that she would become the love of my life, and would be my anchor to home throughout the war. Most of that time, as you will read, we would be apart. After the war was over, we would marry, and sixty years later we would celebrate our diamond wedding anniversary. As a child, I thought Gloucester was the centre of the world, now it actually was for me.

Knowledge Is Power

One bleak February morning in 1942, we travelled by train in company with other naval-parties, from Devonport to Liverpool. Once there, we would embark on the troop ship SS Empress of Scotland. She was formerly named Empress of Japan. At that time, it was not allowed for a ship's name to be changed, but Winston Churchill declared it to be a nonsense for her to be named, after what he regarded to be a traitor nation. She once used to ply the North Pacific route, where she was regarded as being the finest, largest, and fastest passenger ship, accommodating 1,200, in a mix of the various passenger classes. Now stripped of her Canadian Pacific livery and painted 'battleship grey', her troop-decks would accommodate around 4,400 personnel.

Arriving at the dockside, my first impression was that she looked a little old fashioned, having a tall mast forward and another aft, and with three large funnels. I later found out that the after funnel was a dummy, a ventilation shaft for the engine rooms and galleys. No longer were there luxury fittings, we would sleep in bunks suspended by chains in tiers of three, if I remember rightly. As usual the officer's quarters were separated from ours, and they didn't suffer quite the same privations that we did. Being in the Navy I was used to this. I did admire the bravery of crews of Merchant Navy ships, such as this one. We would be aboard for a few days enduring a one-way crossing to New York, but they had to withstand many months of such crossings, aboard a ship which would be the pre-eminent target in most convoys - a trophy for any U-boat captain.

I had got to know others of our party during the train journey and the ocean crossing. This naval party, totalling over 50, was a mix of senior and junior ratings, and a variety of different specialisations. We were obviously to form a crew for a small ship, but the low numbers of gunnery or torpedo branch specialisations made it pretty obvious it was not to be an escort vessel. Speculation was rife that we would crew one of the host of 'landing ships tank', or LSTs as they were known, which were being constructed. This was confirmed on arrival when we met our officers, until then a chief petty officer coxswain had been in overall charge of us. If he knew our fate, he didn't let on to us. His attitude seemed to be 'knowledge is power' and he wanted to retain it for himself. He proved to be both rigid and narrow minded, more attuned to the regime of a battleship than to that of a 'little ship'.

New York was an eye-opener for us Brits arriving from blacked-out and bomb-damaged cities, such as Plymouth and Liverpool. Here the skyscrapers blazed with lights, traffic noisy with hooting and honking filled the streets, and there seemed to be an abundance of everything that we lacked at home.

Along with many other groups of British service personnel we were accommodated in what was known at the time as HMS Asbury. Part of the 'lease lend agreement', this establishment was formed from two hotels, the New Monterey and the Berkeley Carteret, located in Asbury Park area, New Jersey. It was used as a transit camp for those like us who had come to collect ships under construction, or those being refitted.

The floating bathtub, and the ships with no name

Towards the end of March 1943 we had confirmation we were to crew an LST which was already in commission as the USS LST-163, but to be transferred to the Royal Navy on the 29th March. We would join her at New Orleans, Louisiana. Joining her entailed for us a rail journey of over 1,300 miles. This could be quite an exciting adventure, we thought. We had watched Hollywood movies while at Astbury, some of which featured journeys by long distance Pullman express sleeper-trains.

Our experience proved quite different. Arriving at Pennsylvania station, New York, we were packed tightly like sardines, shoulder to shoulder in a couple of long rail-cars. The journey took about forty hours and involved two whole nights. We sometimes rocked slowly along the track and at other times were halted for half an hour or so in sidings, enabling priority freight trains to pass. Some were trailing flatbeds, laden with tanks and other military vehicles, en-route to the ports for shipping to the various theatres of war. Other long trains were carrying livestock or agricultural products. Guns and butter, they lifted America out of depression, and along with lease-lend they helped the USA to become the post-war super-power. Scrolling past the carriage window seemed to be endless reels of changing vistas – mountain views, pine forest, placid lakes, small towns with houses flying the stars and stripes, junk yards and cypress swamps. I soon tired of looking out but found sleep difficult. Rounding bends, I could see the steam-belching locomotive in front of us and could hear the mournful sound of the horn as we rattled over crossings with flashing lights and the clanging sound of warning bells.

We arrived at New Orleans tired and cramped after the long journey and were taken to the navy yard on the Mississippi river delta. At the jetty, LST-163 seemed small, with her upper-works level with the jetty because of the low tide. The huge bow doors were open and the ramp was lowered, thus we could gaze down into the cavernous tank deck. "She looks like a floating bathtub" remarked our leading chef.

An advance party of our crew were already on the ship, they had taken her over from the US navy. The party included most of our officers and the technical department heads. They had been familiarised with the US pattern equipment and were ready to pass on to us the knowledge they had gained.

200 LSTs had been ordered for our navy as part of the lease-lend programme and another 800 were built for the US Navy; they were the result of a joint requirement, and an agreed design for both navies. The all-welded construction enabled these ships to be fabricated wherever there was capacity. These fabrications could then be transported to wherever final assembly would be. It was said that Winston Churchill had made a rough sketch, for a ship which could have made the withdrawal of troops from the beaches at Dunkirk easier and would have enabled vehicles and equipment to be saved, rather than be abandoned. Our ship was the Mk. 2 version and was designed to carry a load up to 1,900 tons, which could comprise of around 18 to 22 tanks, or a mix of other vehicles and equipment. She also had berths for 217 troops.

We had a deadline to meet, and much training to undergo before we sailed to Halifax, Nova Scotia; a sea voyage of around 1,700 miles.

A convoy was being formed to depart Halifax bound for Liverpool on the 18th of May, this was known as SC 131 a convoy for ships having a slow speed. Our top speed was 12 knots but at this speed we used too much fuel to achieve the 2,700 miles crossing, thus our convoy speed would be about 9 knots. The weather for much of the voyage was rough. The ships were climbing to mountainous crests before crashing down their reverse slope only then to bury their noses before rising to meet their next mountain to climb. In the back of our minds was the fear that these hastily constructed vessels would not withstand the continual battering. It had been known for these, and other ships with similar type of hull, to suffer with splits which caused some to founder. Rescue from the sea in these conditions would be difficult or perhaps impossible. It was for this reason that we did not arrive at Liverpool until the 31st of May. We had an escort which averaged around four or five corvettes or destroyers, I say 'averaged' because the escort would change over every five days, probably because our slow speed would limit their range also, owing to the fact that they had to zigzag, as sheep-dogs do, to keep the 31 ships they were shepherding in some sort of order and together. They probably had to then

rendezvous with a convoy in-bound for Halifax, on their way back to refuel, and escort it in to harbour.

Our convoy arrived intact at Liverpool, possibly that was because our escorts had protected us so well.

Rose Marie, I'm always dreaming of you

This ungainly bathtub had to become more than just a home for us, she had to become a war-winner. This ship, along with others of her type would enable our armies to land in strength on foreign shores. She was unlike any warship any of us had served aboard, not only in looks, but also with aspects regarding buoyancy and trim. The stoker petty officer said that she was more akin to the floating dock he had once served on. She was flat-bottomed, this enabled her to float in a few feet of water, giving her the ability to land troops and vehicles onto a shelving beach, but also, she had to be capable of being trimmed, to enable her to make an ocean crossing, without being blown off course by the wind, or tossed about like a matchbox in heavy seas. Peter Spear, the chef, he who had called her a bathtub, and the Jack dusty (Navy slang for stores assistant) Jeff Turnbull, had become my run ashore oppos. There was not any ulterior motive for me, only because we seemed to jell as personalities. We poked fun at ourselves, and at situations we found ourselves in, and we had a similar sense of humour. I say ulterior motive, because the little extra treats a chef or a store-man was in a position to provide, could sometime seem like manna from heaven. We didn't know then, that we would serve together on this ship the whole time it was in commission, and that we would remain friends after the war's end. I had endeared myself to Peter by pointing out to him that he had sewn his 'officers cook' badge, to both of his jacket sleeves instead of only to the right arm-sleeve. He said he thought he should do that, as he was issued with two of the badges. I suppose there was some excuse for him to think like that, because just a few weeks before joining up as a HO rating he was working as a pastry cook in a seaside hotel.

I think during my time on this ship we had four different captains, all of them RN reserves, all Lieutenant Commander by rank, and we had over those three years the same number of coxswains. Other officers and crew-members would be replaced because of ill-health or on promotion, or some for any other reason 'their lordships' deemed necessary. Some would serve years, and others only months. At any one time probably only a third of the crew were navy regulars, the others would be a mix of HO's, volunteer reserves and RNR's.

These ships were carthorses not thoroughbred racers. They couldn't jump fences or win any races but they could haul a mixed load and run it up onto a shallow beach on a rising tide offload and be able to pull themselves off into deeper water by using the great big winch, which took up most of the space on the quarterdeck. We would drop our stern anchor before beaching ready for when we needed to pull ourselves off, to avoid us becoming stranded like a beached whale once the tide turned.

There would no scrubbing of wood-planked decks or brass-work to be polished, no bugle calls or marine band and no sunset ceremony. We just pulled the flag up, if someone had remembered to put it there in the first place.

We had no name – just the numerals 163 painted in white either side of the bow, very handy to enable the mail, or stores-boats to identify which one, of perhaps a dozen of identical LSTs, these items had to be delivered to.

At anchor (at whatever port we happened to be) sometimes we would be waiting to load, or waiting already loaded, when the troops or tank crews eager to get off, would often be happier to meet the enemy than to suffer the seasickness the effects of an unsettled sea caused to those in a flat-bottomed box.

One sultry afternoon we three musketeers, had sat in a honky-tonk bar in New Orleans drowning our sorrows, while listening to an old black guy with a careworn face, his lips pursed, while coaxing a haunting tune, melodious and sad,

out of his battered sax. He was good enough as a musician to play on Broadway or down 'tin pan alley', but he was going nowhere, just playing to we three sailors as we stoked ourselves up with enough booze to sustain ourselves during the forthcoming voyage to Halifax. This was the 'black quarter', and we were the only white men in this shanty.

There was no racism practiced in the Royal Navy, at least if there was, I never detected it. If you had a bar and some beer, we would drink it. Anyway, the point of all this waffle is – Jack dusty said "We should call her the Mary Rose", referring to our ship with no name. Pete retorted, "You clown, she is lying off Portsmouth upside down below a hundred feet of water, along with the remains of all who were aboard". This showed the level our conversation would sink to once the warm beer had worked its magic. "Rose Marie", said I. It was one of the tunes the musician had included in his medley. Thereafter, when talking amongst ourselves, this is what we called our old grey bathtub, with which you might say we had a love-hate relationship. The next morning, our heads pounding, we would swear that the beer must have been below par, or the craw-fish pie and the fillet gumbo was off; anything, but that we had imbibed too much.

At those beachheads along the coast of Africa and at Palermo and other landing places on Sicily, as well as Anzio, Italy, and at the Mulberry harbours and beaches of Normandy, at all of these places, mayhem and death could be happening, all around us. I had seen other landing ships blown-up, broken-up and shot-up, but I don't recall a single member of our crew being injured, unlike my previous experience. Rose Marie brought us through it all, totally unscathed.

The living quarters for the 60 officers and men of the ships company were situated aft. Our junior rates mess was one big open space. It was furnished with the usual tables, long benches, and pull-down bunks. We led a Spartan-like existence. At sea, some bunks would be in use by those who had come off watch. Other mess-members would be on watch, while the remainder would be either having their meal, or be trying to play card games, or attempting to concentrate reading a book. All of this, while our little world was perhaps, rolling or pitching about, on an angry sea. The senior rates mess was a curtained off area of the same compartment. Probably so that they didn't have to watch the lions feed.

The portholes of the bathroom looked out astern, so you were able to watch the ship's foaming wake disappearing into the distance while you cleaned your teeth and dreamed of home. One forenoon during one of our cross-channel shuttles between the Solent and Normandy I entered the bathroom and through the porthole I saw, looming up on us, the bow of the LST which was supposed to be in-line astern and keeping a safe distance. She was just a few feet away, and about to ram us. Those in the bathroom had their heads down, while washing in the sink. My shout of alarm probably saved their lives. This collision resulted in us spending a few days in the dockyard while the stern was patched up. They didn't bother to iron out all the bumps and scratches, they just slapped some red lead and battleship grey over them, and we carried on regardless. You may be aware that there are fifty shades of grey, our battleship grey is a couple of shades lighter than the US navy dull grey, so it was something of a mismatch, but it made Rose Marie stand out from the crowd. Not being a royal yacht, or the admiral's barge, little notice was ever taken of us. During my three years of service aboard her I can never recall the ship having an admiral's inspection or any ceremonial event. At the end of the commission we handed Rose Marie back to the US Navy. They didn't worry about the odd bump and scrape either, as they had plenty of their own war-weary, blown-up, or shot-up LSTs. By all accounts our Rose Marie was sold on after the war, bumps and scrapes et-al, to a merchant-shipping company in Singapore. They no doubt renamed her Rosie Lee.

The Atlantic crossing had been slow, but being in convoy we had no chance to put the ship through her paces; or for us the crew, to train how to load and unload the cart, as you might say. We had carried some sort of load with us, but not military vehicles. We proceeded to a Scottish loch, where a suitable area had been selected for LSTs to practice. This loch had a range of the types of shore that we could expect to encounter, wherever their lordships had in mind to send us. We would also have chance to test-fire our anti-aircraft armament. It would be usual for us to be in a protected convoy during amphibious operations, so we would not expect attacks by surface vessels.

During our recent Atlantic crossing we had been placed at the rear of the convoy, probably to enable us to have a clear field of fire against air attack, and we could help protect the convoy against any U-boat that might try to enter the rear of the convoy on the surface. Jock Brodie, an HO stoker mechanic, born and raised in the back streets of Glasgow, said that this ocean voyage, apart from the Atlantic crossing by troopship, had been the fastest he'd ever travelled on water and he had spent ten years afloat. He told us that since a lad of fourteen he had worked in the engine room of the Prince Edward, a steam driven paddle steamer that plied Loch Lomond. She carried day-trippers, who in the main would be those that could afford a day, or a weekend break from Glasgow's noise and bustle. For those ten years he had voyaged about 30 miles in each direction, between Balloch and Ardui, but had only plodded along at 8 knots maximum. Looking at him you would think the oil and grease stained overalls he wore now, were the same pair that he had worn for all of those years! Despite his appearance, he proved, with time to be one of the ship's best and most reliable engineers.

While in Scotland we practised both loading through our bow doors, then using the elevator to transfer the vehicles to the upper deck for stowage. Once in place they had to be secured with chains to the deck in case we should encounter rough weather. Tanks would only be carried on the tank deck, not on the upper deck. While those vehicles were being secured, the cavernous tank deck would be filled with tanks, or with other vehicles, and they also would be secured. Being a torpedo-man on a ship without torpedoes, I was part of the electrical party and as such had a variety of equipment to familiarise myself with. I became proficient at operating the panel which provided the power and means for opening the huge bow doors, and also for the raising and lowering of the hinged vehicle ramp. I seem to possess the knack and judgement required for this task – you might say that I had found my niche. This was a job many of the others didn't seem to want to do, so it became my role. Four different captains had Rose Marie and during those three years she had only one bow door operator. None of these captains wanted either the bow door, the ramp or its mechanism to foul-up and not be able to be lowered or raised. Their object, and the desire of the whole crew, was to get the ship to which-ever location the beach master directed us to, and to rid ourselves of our cargo through the doors and across the ramps. As soon as possible when this was done, we would raise the ramp and secure the doors while the ship was winching herself off the beach, then, to be ready to pull up the anchor and head away from whatever mayhem was, or could be happening. It was in everyone's interest, as other LSTs could be bobbing about, while waiting their turn to beach. Around us other LSTs sometimes fouled their doors, or had problems raising the ramp for whatever reason, and could be stuck like beached whales and exposed on the shore. The switch-gear in the panel could be temperamental, as could the door or ramp mechanism. I would service, grease, and oil ours often; the same way I was trained to do as a motor mechanic, servicing cars, or as a torpedo-man caring for the torpedo launching tubes and for the torpedoes themselves. Our equipment never failed. I had a few 'close shaves' as you might say but was always able to rectify any problem before it became a disaster. I won no awards but Pete the chef, would sometimes slip me an egg sandwich, or other treat, while I was at my station!

From my position at the panel I could only see what was happening ahead through the open bow doors as I watched the troops and vehicles departing. They were usually as eager to go as we were to see them gone. I remember one occasion when a frightened soldier hung onto me and said he couldn't bring himself to go. I spoke to him reassuringly while I was readying myself to raise the ramp. I told him that we were all scared and that our ship would have to head back, reload and be back here again the next morning. I also said, once you get moving you will be okay. With that he seemed to pull himself together, he grabbed his weapon and ran across the ramp, just before I raised it. I have no doubt he went on to perform as well as any other man did. I only remember one occasion that a man was so frightened and unable to move we had to take him back with us. Only that one, out of the many thousands of the men I had watched as they departed through our bow doors.

I mentioned our defensive armament which fortunately we didn't use too often in direct defence of ourselves, but only as part of a general barrage against enemy aircraft that might be attacking the whole landing area. We had one gunner, 'Teresa' Green, who was particularly trigger happy. He would blaze away furiously at anything that dared to fly in the sky above us, be it bird or aircraft. When it happened to be allied aircraft he would have to be restrained. Fortunately, his aim was poor and he never scored any hits. We didn't mind the sound of our gun-fire, it was a reassurance that we were not just a defenceless sitting duck. The armament depot thought Rose Marie saw more action than did any of the other LSTs, but that was due to Leading Seaman Green. Before the 'D' Day landings he was promoted to petty officer to replace our quartermaster. Jack dusty said that had been done to make it safer for the RAF.

Mentioning our Jack dusty, Jeff Turnbull, reminds me that he was the most resourceful person I have ever met. As store-man his main duties when we were in harbour were the posting of our mail, and trying to track down any mail that had been sent to us. It was not always an easy task, because often we would be shuttling tanks and equipment from one remote area to another. To assist in this he had acquired a battered bike, known in our parlance as a 'pusser's red devil' the navy-issue equivalent of the postman's bike, but not always painted red. Jeff's other task was to purchase fresh food supplies from wherever he could, at most reasonable cost. Generally he used a bartering system. He would peddle off to a local village, or a scrubland farm, taking with him goods to barter with from our stores. It may surprise you to know that in these hot, arid, desert areas the inhabitants highly valued the navy-issue black woollen balaclava-type hats or the white woollen submarine-issue sweaters, above anything else; probably because at night the temperature dropped quite markedly. We didn't have these items in our stores therefore Jack would purloin them, usually from any escort vessel that had served in the North Atlantic or exchange them for items we had in abundance. He would often return from his bartering forays ashore carrying a live chicken or two or leading a small goat. We had an HO rating aboard who had been a butcher when a civilian. He would slaughter the animal which would then be left hanging from the guardrails, over the ships side, to allow the blood to drain.

I will say this; it was not the practice of the Navy to take anything without payment, unlike some forces of some other countries that had passed through these areas.

Gold at Normandy

Despite there being what you might think to be a great number of these purpose-built ships, LSTs were in great demand. As the allied armies advanced along the North African coast, then invaded Sicily and later landed, at Anzio. Italy, it was the same LSTs that were used. They would be withdrawn from one area to be sent on to the next as the war's progress demanded. For those reasons, we departed from the Mediterranean in February 1944, initially bound for the River Clyde to have a short refit. During this refit our ship was fitted with stretcher-racks to provide berths for 144 wounded. Later we were sent to Invergordon and to the shores of the Moray Firth. There we would train with others for the forthcoming 'second front', as it was known. We did not know it then, but the forthcoming landings would be at Normandy, France.

To be in readiness for this, along with seven other LSTs of our 5th flotilla, we arrived at Portsmouth in mid-April. To the best of my knowledge around 60 LSTs were to be used for 'operation Neptune', the code name for those landings.

My recollections of this are best taken from a recording I made in 1984 for the memorial service at Gosport to mark the 40th anniversary of D-day. The text was later printed in a publication titled, 'Gosport remembers D-day'. This was compiled by Gosport historians, Lesley A. Burton and my late wife, Beryl F. Peacey.

We were at anchor, during a cold wet and windy weekend, at the beginning of June. We were one unnamed ship, amongst a host of other ships of different types, that were also at anchor between Stokes Bay and the Isle of Wight. We were laden with tanks, military vehicles, ammunition, and British soldiers. Most of the soldiers had become sea-sick, and longed to be off and away from the ship. I remember one of them saying to me "I don't know how you can face going backwards and forwards, between Gosport and Normandy. Let me get ashore where I can dig myself in". I have forgotten my reply but in essence, it was `rather you than me'.

After what seemed an endless wait for a lull to occur in this unusually rough weather, we weighed anchor and headed for yet another beachhead. As usual we hope to offload quickly and return to home shores. When `beaching stations' were ordered, I was ready to open the bow doors and lower the ramp as soon as the panel light-indicators dictated. The rumble of tanks, and the engine noise of other vehicles leaving above the sound of gunfire, was music to my ears. I had no idea at the time, it was just another landing to us, but it turned out to we were at` Gold' beach, and by luck, LST163, our Rose Marie, continued to lead a charmed life. On our return to Gosport after each crossing, we would take on our next load either at Stokes Bay, Beach Street or my favourite area, the Hardway. For the next three months we continued to ply back and forth between Normandy and Gosport carrying essential supplies, and on the return journey we

brought back wounded soldiers. Our tank deck had been fitted with stretchers. I often acted as a theatre orderly in order to help the medical corps surgeons while they conducted operations on urgent cases. Any limbs that were amputated had to be disposed of over the ships side. Arriving at the Hardway we would discharge the wounded to the care of the military ambulances which were waiting there. We also brought back many German prisoners; some were arrogant and surly, and once or twice I had a bowl of soup thrown over me. That was a silly thing for a prisoner who was being treated well, to do. The military escorts would note who these individuals were, and eventually they would be disciplined.

Leaving on a jet plane

By September 1944 we had completed over twenty return crossings between Gosport and Normandy. These shuttle trips could be quite hazardous, not only due to the number of other ships which were doing similar crossings, some of them employing little or no lane discipline, but also we would suffer the occasional strafing run by a Focke-wulfe 190, or whatever. Once the Mulberry harbours were in place we would berth on one of them; the advantage of that was that we could carry our maximum load, as we were not subject to the rise and fall of the tides and therefore we had no need to adjust our trim which made the turn-around quicker.

We were withdrawn from these duties to prepare us for the forthcoming operation Zipper. The ultimate aim of which was the liberation of Singapore and the Malaysian peninsular; but of course we didn't know that until much later. This would involve us being fitted to cope better with tropical climate. After this was completed, in company with six other LSTs, we departed Milford Haven on the 19th December as part of a convoy. We carried, chained and secure on our upper deck, a landing craft tank (as they were known) quite a large vessel, 160' long, with a 30' beam, with the capacity to carry up to five tanks, to off-load through her bow ramp to the beach. Christmas day, as we crossed the Bay of Biscay, we were rolling and pitching about, while trying to keep together as a convoy. This was not easy to do as some of the other LSTs did not have the standard size propellers, which made keeping in formation difficult. Once we had passed through the straits of Gibraltar it became plain sailing in the calm of the Mediterranean. We had transited the Suez Canal and were preparing to enter Port Said when we, the Rose Marie, suffered a failure of our steering gear. The other LSTs had to veer away to avoid collision, but we hit the side of one of the merchant ships which had found it impossible to manoeuvre away fast enough. The resulting bumps and scrapes to our bow had to be patched up primed in red lead, and as usual, finished with a coat of battleship grey, another trophy which added to our look of dishevelment.

The convoy arrived at Calcutta on the 31st January 1945 and we moored alongside a jetty in order to carry out routine self-maintenance and to work on the steering gear which had failed while at Port Said (a common problem for LSTs to suffer).

A treat for us, before we were to load troops and their vehicles bound for Malaya, was to be a showing of the films 'We'll Meet Again' and 'Rhythm and Serenade', both of which starred Vera Lynn. The films would be viewed on consecutive evenings under the upper-deck awning where it would be cool and airy: the screen would be rigged against bridge super-structure.

Before the film started we had a special meal of curried chicken and rice along with two bottles of Indian beer per man, making it a rare treat for us. Vera Lynn had been here in India when en- route to Burma back in 1944, and we later would transport troops who had seen her in the ENSA concerts. She became known as the 'forces sweetheart': the result of a poll taken to find servicemen's favourite 'entertainer', and she had become a link to home for many of us. I knew from Beryl's letters to me that she had seen and enjoyed both films and like many others with loved ones away serving in the Armed Forces, she would listen to the Sunday evening BBC Radio Show, 'Sincerely Yours'. Vera Lynn would read out messages from loved ones, which all could empathise with. It would be more likely for us to hear

'Starlight Express' a short programme the BBC broadcast several times throughout each 24-hour period to enable servicemen hear it, whichever time zone they happened to be in. Even Jock Brodie had changed from his usual grease-stained overalls into regulation 'night clothing' for the occasion. We were familiar with the songs of both movies, in fact most of us knew the lyrics by heart. One of our officers possessed an old HMV wind-up gramophone. Our new

Captain thought it good for our morale, as indeed it was, for the records to be played over the ship's loudspeaker system as the ship ploughed her way through what seemed an endless ocean. The Quartermaster and his side-boy would have their work cut out with winding the handle, so

sometimes the music would slow down and Vera's usual clear English diction would become distorted, but overall her ethereal dulcet voice lifted our spirits and made life easier. I remember, with the ambience created by those movies, and with Vera Lynn not being the usual film-star glamour girl but more like the girl next door, she became our own personal sweetheart those evenings. The stardust she scattered even touched Jock Brodie; with him saying it reminded him of the September 'Sunset Cruises' on the tranquil Lomond. He thereupon took out a packet of Woodbines and offered them to all around... and that had never been known before!

Eventually around 50 LSTs were deployed for this operation, the landings in Malaysia; some to land at Port Dickson, and we together with the others were to beach at Port Swettenham.

We had called at another place when en-route to Calcutta to deliver the landing craft, but unfortunately there was no crane at the jetty with which to lift her off. After much scratching of heads, a plan was hatched. This plan involved welding steel girders, like railway lines, leading from our upper deck at an angle down to sea-level; greasing them, then flooding the trim tanks on that side, before releasing the securing chains and encouraging the craft to slide down the rails and into the sea. You can probably imagine the splash and the mini tidal-wave this caused. But it worked!

You may wonder what routine we worked, and what work we did, during this build up to the invasion of Malaysia. Well, we were not just sitting around while waiting for this to happen; the troops (most of those we transported were from the Indian 25th Division) and their vehicles, had to be in position for the invasion itself. On one of our return trips, inbound to Calcutta and still some 250miles offshore in the Bay of Bengal, we suffered a complete loss of propulsion and power generation. Our tame grease monkey, Jock, would regale us with one of his Loch Lomond 'sea stories' while he worked on deck to repair some mechanical contraption that was necessary to get us underway again. He told us of those times on the old Prince Edward, when he would be feverishly wielding his spanner down below while those day-trippers on the upper-deck, being oblivious to the situation, would think this peaceful interlude spent floating without power to the paddles, was a planned part of the experience.

Our two V12 diesels and all three generators had failed because of some gremlin in the system. This caused us to wallow about at the mercy of whatever weather was on offer. Fortunately, the winds remained light and the ocean calm, because it was another two days before the problem was fixed. In the meantime, with no electrical power our 90-day frozen food supply had become defrosted and was soon declared to be 'not edible' (even for us of the lower order). It was therefore decided that we would 'feed it to the fishes' as they say.

i decided to try my hand at some fishing to catch fresh produce by using our rotten meat as bait. Jack dusty supplied me with the only type of hook he had in his store, not a barbed fishing hook, but one of those that we used when hooking our sun protection awnings to superstructure. I secured the hook to a length of heaving line, baited it with what was once prime beef, and tossed it over the guardrail. Within seconds I had a mighty shark on the hook, or so I thought! This shark had its own way and swallowed it 'hook, line and sinker' as the saying goes. I was left just holding on to that part of the line he didn't swallow. Not one to be thwarted, I repeated the process, as Jack Dusty had plenty of hooks and a freezer full of rancid meat; but this time I attached the hook to a wire rope that I had secured to the outboard end of a hemp-rope.

A shark soon obliged but put up a mighty struggle as we hauled it inboard using the boat's davit hoist. Measuring some eight-foot from snout to tail, this 'white-tip terror shark' threshed about furiously on deck, while we dodged

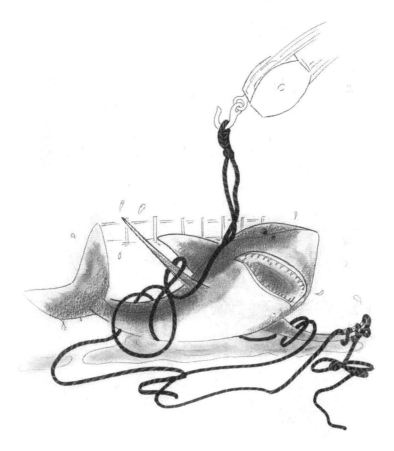

about to avoid its sharp end. 'Teresa' Green, our

quartermaster, shot it from close range using his Lee Enfield rifle; the only time he ever scored a hit on anything he aimed at, mind you the shark's brain was only inches from the rifle's muzzle. You may think this is hard to believe, but when the shark was opened up to remove my hook, the other hook and line were discovered to be inside it! Really astounding, for although in these waters it is not unusual to see a shark or two, word obviously travels fast in the underwater world, within ten minutes of the meat going in, we must have had every shark in the Indian Ocean sampling our menu while we were reduced to 'hard tack' for the next few days.

The weather usually was hot and steamy. We above decks would wear shorts and sandals, with usually a wide brimmed hat for protection against the sun; very little of regular uniform to distinguish one from another. Those who worked below in the engine room would probably wear overalls instead of the shorts. We tended to work a tropical routine when not on watch at sea, but when in harbour we would start early to do our work before the heat of the day. My own role was to work on anything electrical, servicing those motors which powered most things; the capstan, the various pumps and winches, and the motors that powered the elevator, the ramp and the bow doors.

My 'tin hat' I kept hanging near my action-station. The gunners would keep their steel helmets somewhere handy to their weapons, so should we suffer a surprise attack by marauding Japanese aircraft, we were ready.

Our latest coxswain (who had joined the ship before we left the UK) had the 'RN barracks mentality'. If he had held sway, we would wear boots and gaiters and carry gas-masks while we marched about as soldiers do but luckily our first lieutenant kept him on a leash. I will give you an example of his mentality – I had been gifted with a package of quality tea by a Ceylonese army officer, to express his gratitude after I had serviced the troublesome jeep he had driven aboard. (A simple job for me to do, just a quick adjustment to the engine's timing). Anyway, I parcelled the tea in brown paper tied up with string, ready to post home to my mother. I thought it would be a nice present for her because of the rationing and shortages at home. Any item to be sent from the ship would have to pass through the coxswain's office for clearance. I was astonished when he made me remove the string; because it was Navy issue, and not to be used for private purposes. Luckily, Jack dusty came to my aid, as he managed to produce from somewhere a length of Indian army parachute cord. That stumped the coxswain! Jock Brodie, who was in the queue and standing behind me, was grinning from ear to ear like a Cheshire Cat. The cox'n rounded on him in his aggressive bulldog manner. "What are you smirking at?" he bellowed. Jock's reply I have never forgotten, "Simple

people are always happy 'swain, which makes me surprised that you are not forever gleeful".

The dropping of the atomic bombs on the 6th and 9th August resulted in Japan's surrender six days later. The landings went ahead anyway and were totally unopposed. We were employed in that area of Malaysia and around Borneo, Sumatra and Java thereafter; to repatriate those who had been prisoners of war, many of whom were in pitiful condition. We also began withdrawing troops and their equipment from where they were no longer required. At times we were required to send armed landing parties ashore: the aim was to round-up any Japanese soldiers that were still on the islands.   I was not over-keen when I had to do this for two reasons: the first, because it seemed that nobody had told the Japs that the war was over and the word 'surrender' was not in their vocabulary. Secondly, those Japs had been in those places for a long time, they were familiar with the local area and had got themselves pretty well dug in. Apart from those considerations, I didn't think that the service rifle that I had been issued with was the best close-quarter weapon to use in 'jungle warfare', as you might call it. I was pleased therefore, when we were withdrawn in order to take Rose Marie to Singapore. I was more than just happy to let the army do that which they enjoyed doing!

We paid off on the 15th February 1946 at Singapore. My war was over, and now I just wanted to get back home to Bulley and to Beryl Dobbs.

Getting home was not like leaving on a jet plane, the way servicemen would do it these days. As usual we had to wait. We waited until a suitable ship was available – this turned out to be the Devonport based, HMS Loch Eck a fast, anti-submarine frigate of the Loch class. She was rated as 'fast', but like many small ships she could only carry a limited amount fuel. For that reason she would only be able to sail at 12 knots for the long haul back to the UK; so it would not be a high speed dash. The voyage home via Ceylon, Aden and the Suez Canal took her three months; we left Singapore 20th of May and arrived at Devonport the 13th of August. Loch Eck collided with another Royal Naval ship while at Colombo and had to spend all of June under repair. A large number of their crew were HO ratings, all eager to get home to their families and to the civilian jobs which they hoped would still be open to them. It was rumoured that they had been in mutinous mood when it was suggested that their ship would be remaining on station for longer. They got short shrift from the HO ratings of Rose Marie and from us regulars as well. We had been in commission for three years as opposed to their eighteen months. We did learn that during that period she, along with two other ships of her escort group, had been credited with the sinking of three U-boats. "Mind you" said Jack dusty, "I bet we sank a few more pints than they did"

Back Home

Arriving back at Devonport aboard Loch Eck was a wonderful feeling for me, and probably it was for most others on board. The war had touched us all, but not for all in the same way. Peter, Jeff and I vowed we would meet again 'don't know where, don't know when' as it said in one of our favourite Vera Lynn songs, when they, along with all those others who had been called-up to serve for the duration of the hostilities only, would be returning to civilian life They had experienced things that they hadn't volunteered for, but ones they would never forget. They told me in retrospect that many of those memories created by the war did serve to enrich their lives and helped them to cope with the vicissitudes of life that are common to us all. The hostilities had ceased for almost a year, the armistice was signed with Germany 8th May 1945 and the Japanese had surrendered on the 15th August 1945. VE and VJ days had been celebrated by those at home with parties, and people dancing in the streets, but both of these events and the celebrations had passed us by.

For some on board, whose loved ones were either injured or lost to bombing at their homes, or by battle-fighting, it was no doubt a mixture of feelings. I heard that our captain was returning to his work at Trinity House and our first lieutenant to his job at the bank. The coxswain's posting was to a training school, as an instructor, so our loss was their loss! The rest of the reserves and the HO ratings would pick-up with their own careers in civilian life, and no doubt would help to get the country back on its feet after the devastation this war had wrought. Even Jock Brodie, who the engineer officer had tried to convince to sign on as a regular in the Navy, was desperately keen to return to the Prince Edward or to one of those paddle steamers that plied the River Clyde holiday routes. There would be no spoils for the victors, only blood, sweat, toil and tears but at least we were back home.

Before my next posting, whatever that might be, I went back to HMS Defiance to qualify as a UW2 (Underwater Weapons, second class); the specialisation had changed from that known before as a torpedo-man. Not only had its name been changed, but also some new weapon-systems had been introduced to combat the U-boat threat. One of these new introductions, the 'squid', an anti-submarine mortar system, was fitted to the Loch Eck and to the other ships of her class. Using this weapon system assisted with the sinking of the three U-boats, a feat they were so rightly proud of. During the long voyage home I had ample opportunity to study the mortar-mounting, the projectiles and the operating method of the whole system. This knowledge stood me in good stead for the course I now had to take.

On completion of the course I travelled to Beryl's home to enjoy a three week leave period. She was now living at Filton, on the outskirts of Bristol; her father had been promoted and transferred to work and to live there. Their home was a police house at the address where I had been corresponding with Beryl. The lovely letters she had written to me were full of hope and of plans for our future together. She never lost faith that once this war was over there would be a better life for us all. Since her move to Filton she had become the personal secretary to one of the directors of the Bristol Aeroplane Company, at their Filton base. Her fast shorthand skills enabled her to record verbatim the minutes of those meetings of technical complexity: important work, in a company heavily involved with military aircraft production and with important post-war projects, including prototypes for the Bristol Brabazon, a large airliner. It was during my leave that we decided we would get married fairly soon, and toward this end we got the blessing of her parents; we duly announced our engagement on the 4th September 1946.

When I returned to the barracks at Devonport, a large contingent of men were being readied to form the ships company for a cruiser which was soon to depart for the Far East station, and it seemed probable that I was to be one of them. With that in mind we thought it prudent to get married as soon as possible, at least then we would be in receipt of marriage allowance during the expected separation. The wedding was arranged to be held at Huntley church, the church where Beryl's family had worshipped when they lived at Huntley. The date arranged with the clergyman was 7th December.

I had seen on the regulating office notice-board an entitlement notice for 'Marital Leave', so I was confident that my request to the commander would be granted. As is naval practice request-men (and defaulters) have to attend the commanders table, a bit like attending court. I was astonished when the commander almost had a bout of apoplexy. 'No such thing!' he exploded. I had to explain about the notice, but the regulating branch like policemen anywhere are good at covering their own backs, when I looked at the notice-board again that obviously 'out of date' notice had been removed. The result of all this palaver was that I was only granted a 'long weekend leave' – in other words from Friday 4pm until 8am Monday. In this short time I had to travel to Gloucester, get married, honeymoon, and then return to Devonport. Partly due to this limited notice Beryl was unable to get the traditional white dress, but also with rationing still in place few of them were readily available. No such problem for me, most servicemen would marry dressed in their No.1 uniform, but instead of the regular black silk it was usual to wear a white one. Just as well the uniform because any civilian clothing I possessed no longer fitted. The wedding itself was a small, family affair, but a very enjoyable one although all too soon I was saying farewell to my lovely bride! Saying goodbye is not easy or pleasant when a long separation is envisaged. I never had the chance to say goodbye to my father and had always felt a tinge of guilt, when as the man of the house I said goodbye to my mother to go and train for war. I felt guilt then, because I felt excited by the prospect but I had no such feeling now.

The Cold War Years

'Submarines are not for me'

Taken Aback

It was good news for me as I had a posting to the main shore base of the Submarine Service, HMS Dolphin at Gosport; no doubt I would be employed in their torpedo workshop to maintain and service those weapons used by the boats there. I was looking forward to being on a shore base for perhaps eighteen months. It should be the ideal place for Beryl and I to start our married life together, and I knew that with her love of history Beryl would find plenty to get involved with. I felt an attachment to this place and its people and so many of my memories were formed here.

With the benefit of hindsight, I now think fate had intervened by bringing me back to Gosport, the town which had been a welcome sight on our return trips from the beaches and the Mulberry harbours of Normandy. We had used the slipways next to the harbour ferry, or at the Hardway which is further up the harbour almost at the entry to Fareham creek. I didn't know at the time of the Normandy landings that the whole of that amazing enterprise was controlled and directed from the Fort Southwick headquarters, which we were able to see above and behind us at Portsdown as we disembarked either our wounded, or those captured German soldiers destined for the prisoner of war camps; before loading our next cargo of men and vehicles bound for France.

Back in those days none of us aboard the LSTs saw much of the town itself, as Gosport and its surrounds were under tight security. Passes were needed to allow entry, even for those who lived there. The slipways at the Hardway were built by laying concrete blocks over rubble from bomb-damaged Portsmouth buildings. So much rubble was used that the citizens of Portsmouth thought they should lay claim to the area. The roads leading to these slipways had deep, strengthening, concrete laid at their corners, thereby allowing tanks to manoeuvre without ripping up the road's surface. Dredgers had worked for many months to dredge out mud and silt to create a bay, wide and deep enough for the landing ships to beach at the slipways. To shroud this activity from the prying eyes of Luftwaffe reconnaissance aircraft, oil-drums which contained a smoke-generating mixture could be ignited if the need arose. Around the area of Stokes Bay, we could see the concrete hard-standings, used when the reinforced concrete caissons to form the walls of the

Mulberry Harbours were constructed. Gangs of Irish labourers had been employed in that area, but by early June 1944, when we were loaded with troops and waiting anchored just offshore, they were all gone, as of course were the Mulberry harbours as well.

Gosport's role was not so much 'front of house' but more the 'upstairs-downstairs' scenario carrying out behind-the-scenes work. Much of what the Navy needed to be able to move and to fight, was provided from here: oil-fuel, victuals and ammunition, as well as those various trained specialists who manned the ships. The people of Gosport, those friendly welcoming people would open up their homes, and make tea and cakes from their own meagre rations to hand out to those young soldiers of many nationalities waiting to embark. These were men and boys, cheerful on the outside but many harbouring inner doubts and trepidation, as they headed off ultimately to fight their way inland from the beachheads.

I arrived by train at Gosport in February of 1947 on my way to HMS Dolphin. The station, like many other prominent places in this area, had been built with defence in mind, having parapets sited on the roof to give defenders an advantage, mind you that was the reason back in 1841 when the station was built. That defensive advantage was no longer relevant during this last war, because the parapets provided no defence from the incendiary bombs dropped by the Luftwaffe in 1941. Those bombs destroyed the locomotive sheds adjacent and caused some damage to the station. It afforded no defence at all when peace-time austerity caused closure of the railway in 1953. (The outer shell of the station being grade 2 listed, remains to this day; its inside space is now a mix of offices and apartments). Those prisoners-of-war, whom we had shipped back from Normandy, were marched here to board trains bound for the various camps. Many of the ambulances, carrying wounded soldiers brought back by the LSTs, were driven here to the station to pass their patients to the care-providers on the hospital-trains.

Dolphin is at Fort Blockhouse, the oldest fortified position still in active military service anywhere in the UK. The base is sited on a narrow land peninsular, and faces across the harbour entrance to Old Portsmouth. Spithead and the Solent are to the south and Haslar Creek, where the submarines berth, is to the north. The fort became the home base of the submarine service in 1905, and since then has been known as HMS Dolphin.

During the normal joining routine I reported to the regulating office. They informed me that my course would start on the next Monday. Taken aback, I asked "What course?" "Your Submarine course, of course", was the answer. I was convinced that there had been a mistake and I had been under the impression that submariners were volunteers! But no, it seemed that there had been a mass exodus from the Navy after the war, not only by those called-up to serve for the war's duration, but also by many regulars whose service should have expired during the war years and who had now left. My own specialisation was in short supply. The electrical branch was formed by using those who had worked in the electrical department of ships not fitted with torpedoes. I thought that I would be one of those but was disappointed to find that because I had completed the UW course I could not now become an electrician. The submarine service would now be the arm of the Navy most likely to use torpedoes as its primary weapon, and this appeared to be their reasoning for my posting.

Brainwashed, the cynic might say

Submarines are not for me was my immediate reaction. I had passed HMS Dolphin countless times while entering or leaving harbour and had seen the sinister looking submarines alongside the jetties at Haslar Creek. I had read a speech by Winston Churchill which stated 'No other branch of the forces shows more devotion to duty and faces grimmer perils than does the submariner'. I also knew that 79 submarines had been lost by the Navy during the war, and apart from these wartime losses I could still remember the accidental loss of the new submarine Thetis just before the war, so I wondered why men would volunteer to serve in them. Having grown up in the countryside, a lover of the great outdoors so to speak,

I didn't relish the thought of being confined in cramped conditions for long periods without access to fresh air.

Despite these reservations, my training thus far had instilled the need to follow orders without question – brainwashed the cynic might say. I carried my kit to the separate training area known as Dolphin 2 and was directed to a Nissan hut, which would accommodate the training-class. Most of the class-members had already settled in and claimed their bunks, so there was little choice left for me. I could have pulled rank and had the bunk of my choice, because as a leading seaman with five years man's service I was senior to all others in this training class. I had no wish to set myself above the others, being wise enough to know that we were now all starting at level zero. Whatever our previous status might have been, we would now be judged by how we performed as submariners. Apart from me and one other, who was also a UW by specialisation, the rest were all younger and apart from a leading steward, most were able rates, but two others were only aged 18, so were still ordinary seamen. They seemed an eager, happy bunch and were a mix of different specializations (radar, sonar, wireless-telegraphy, underwater weapons, a chef and the leading steward). All were volunteers apart from me.

Introducing ourselves to each other by name and by nickname, there would be little formality; our Instructor, a CPO coxswain, gave us an introductory speech to let us know the form the course would take, and what he expected from us. He told us he would explain how a submarine operated and show us certain system-layouts on his chalk board, then he would take us down to a submarine at the jetty, to show it to us 'in the flesh', so to speak; but, before any of this would happen, he would take us aboard a submarine to walk through it and give us a feel for how and where we would live and work. He told us that later, during the course, we would go out for a day-trip aboard one of the submarines to carry out a few evolutions, so we could put the theory into practice. The submarine that we toured was Scotsman, a boat of the S class, the most numerous of any submarine-class ever ordered by the Navy. Sixty-two of them were built, but nineteen had been lost in action against the enemy, or by accident during the war. We didn't know then, that another of the class, Sidon, would be wrecked by an accidental torpedo explosion during 1955, while loading torpedoes at Portland.

The coxswain explained that we would spend two days at the escape training centre adjacent to Dolphin 2 where we would learn the principles of the escape procedure, before carrying out an actual escape by using the Davis escape method. This would be done in the 15' training tank. The thought of it made me apprehensive, but I didn't realise then, that the next time I did the escape procedure, it would be in the 100' tank and by using the free ascent method which was introduced in 1954.

On the 12ᵗʰ January, 1950, the submarine Truculent was rammed and sunk in the Medway estuary. Many of those who were trapped in the submarine on the sea-bed managed to escape using the Davis method, although when the Truculent was salvaged ten bodies were found of those who didn't escape. Unfortunately that escape was carried out before a would-be rescue ship was in position above, ready to take them aboard. Many of those who managed to escape were lost to exposure due to the cold conditions, and by being swept away from the proximity of the collision. Sixty-four men died in this awful accident; as usual lessons had to be learned. An immersion suit was introduced after then, to enable those who reach the surface after escaping to survive the cold and to keep them afloat, and by the provision of an automatic light, to indicate their position to rescuers.

After listening to a general talk about the escape procedure we were taken in groups of ten, to sit in the re-compression chamber. This would artificially reproduce conditions at 200' below the sea. Being under pressure felt uncomfortably hot and our voices became high pitched and squeaky, but it did serve to sort out those who would become claustrophobic, and therefore unsuitable to serve in submarines. Next, we donned the oxygen re-breather set and entered the water at the top of the tank, so we could get comfortable with breathing under water through the face-mask. Once the instructor was satisfied we could do this, eight of us at a time, we entered the escape chamber which was ready to flood and had the twill trunk already rigged, in preparation. The purpose of this trunk was to hold captive the compartment air as it became compressed due to the flooding. Once the pressure had equalised with the sea pressure outside the escape hatch could be opened, then each of us in turn would duck under the trunk and allow the buoyancy in the automatic pressure-relieving life jacket to give us a speedy ascent to the surface. The speed of this ascent could be slowed by using the drogue fitted to the suit's front – but it wasn't necessary to use this in the mere fifteen foot ascent in the tank.

Most of the class would need to do a short conversion course here at Dolphin to bring their specialisation in line with the requirements of the submarine-branch. Myself, and the other UW rates would spend time aboard Scotsman, to learn how torpedoes are handled, loaded, and fired. The Mark 8 torpedoes themselves are standard throughout the Navy. At the end of the two-month course, we would not be qualified as a submariner. We would go to our first submarine to gain three month's experience, before taking part 3 of the training-course. This would be carried out to the satisfaction of the boat's first lieutenant before being allowed to wear the submariners badge.

I enjoyed the course and liked the Instructor's informal manner, but he tolerated no lack of attention, or excuses, and would patiently go through every aspect of a systems operation, until both he himself, and the course member were confident that it was fully understood. His reasoning was that every crew member had to be relied on to do the right thing, as quite often they could be alone in an area or compartment, when action needed to be taken. Two of those on the course were thought not suitable to serve on submarines and were returned to general service, and the one person who panicked while doing the escape procedure, was also deemed to be unsuitable. For myself, although not a volunteer, I was determined to pass both courses as there seemed to be a sense of purpose about submarines and with those crew members I had met so far.

Under the 'Iron Curtain'

The term 'the cold war' has been attributed to the address Churchill as a private citizen, gave to those at the Westminster College at Fulton, Missouri, in 1946. His speech titled 'The sinews of peace' was aimed at a wider audience than this. Within it he mentioned 'the special relationship', a term often used by our government after then. This so-called 'war' has been America's longest, and most costly war – not in human casualties, but in capital outlay. During the 1950s almost half of the US federal budget, and most of their foreign aid spending was directed towards defence, as part of an overall strategic concept. This led to an arms race between the west, in the form of the NATO alliance, and the Soviet Union together, after 1955, with their Warsaw Pact allies. Competing factions, and both of them professing to be 'anti-imperialist'.

Our submarine service had to be readied to meet the Soviet threat, so towards this end the majority of our 'T' and `A' class boats were either streamlined or converted, to make them stealthier and faster.

The role of these boats would be to exercise with NATO forces to gain that expertise needed to meet this threat, or to carry out Intelligence gathering patrols by going under 'the iron curtain' in the Barents Sea; especially in that area close to the Kola peninsula, where the Pechanga naval base is sited.

I was pleased that my first boat, Trespasser, was based at Dolphin, she was not one of those boats selected to be either streamlined, or to be converted, even though she was of all welded construction. I was pleased because when we were not at sea, I was able to look for somewhere where Beryl and I could live. She was as keen to move down to Gosport as I was to have her here. Others on the boat were renting properties locally, but when I found out at what cost, I thought it would make sense to purchase a house of our own. My policy with my pay during the war had been to spend half, and save the other half whenever was possible. Beryl too, had not spent her pay frivolously, so between the two of us our savings were considerable for working class people of our ages. My pay had increased, due to the payment known as 'hard-lying money' that submariners received to help compensate for sub-standard accommodation, and generally poor living conditions. This would be a help when applying for a mortgage because in that era any earnings that one's wife received were not taken into account. I called at Durstons, an estate agency, to obtain the price and their availability of houses. Seeing that a naval rating in uniform had entered his office, the agent pretended to be busy at his desk and was ignoring me for some time. I waited impatiently for a few minutes and then I tapped on his desk. He looked up, and irritably asked, "What do you want?" I am sure if I was dressed as an officer his reaction would have been different. He seemed astounded to hear that I wanted to buy a house, rather than to rent one. He asked "Do you realise that you would need a large deposit?" When I asked if £500 would be enough his demeanour changed immediately, because that was almost half the price of the average house. "Sit down sir" he said. He took me by car to view the few properties he had on his books, some were old houses close to the ferry which I discounted immediately; probably just as well that I did because they had to be demolished a few years later. Then he showed me some small bungalows, off of Anne's Hill Road, to which in annoyance I retorted, "I said a house not a bungalow". Eventually I was shown a semi-detached house at Carnarvon Road, a nice property in good condition, which I thought would be ideal for us. When Beryl travelled down to Gosport the next weekend, she was as delighted as I was with the prospect of owning the house, so we agreed to buy it. We stayed at a hotel in the high street close to the ferry. On the Sunday, before she had to take the train back home to Bristol, we went by ferry across the harbour so we could look at the teacher-training college at Portsmouth. Beryl intended to enquire of them about studying to become a school-teacher, once she had made the move to here.

Come below and dive the submarine

Trespasser as my first posting was a good experience. Attached to Dolphin to carry out a training role, she would take classes of various specialities out for sea-training. Therefore, we would carry out many of those routines of submarine practice on a regular basis. Quite often she would be 'day running', leaving harbour early to be in position before whatever surface ships involved in that day's exercises would arrive. Before 'harbour stations for leaving harbour' was announced, the submarine would have been prepared for sea with many of her systems already checked. The first lieutenant had calculated the trim and made any adjustments required to the water levels of the various trim-tanks. This, when done correctly, would enable the submarine to be in a neutral buoyancy state, once the ballast tanks were flooded when diving. Being in this state it should either prevent us from sinking out of control, like a stone; or from being unable to submerge and left, floundering, on the surface.

Leaving the harbour we would be in 'passage routine', with the main vent cotter-pins in position, this to prevent any accidental flooding of the ballast tanks. To all intents and purposes, when in this state, we were not unlike a surface-ship. By the time we reached the Outer Spit Buoy the mooring wires and ropes would have been stowed under the casing, and the deck-crew would have gone below into the submarine. Propulsion now changed to using the main engines, rather than the two electric-powered main motors, these had been used until we had exited the mouth of the harbour, in case of any emergency, because the main engines are not designed to go astern. The boat could then be opened-up in preparation for diving. Part of this procedure was the removal of cotter-pins from the main vents. The first lieutenant (or the 'Jimmy' as he was known by all, except for the captain, who would refer to him as 'number one') in company with the outside ERA (engine room artificer with responsibility for all machinery outside of the engine room) would inspect the boat from forward to aft, checking that all hatches and valves were in the correct state. Once they were satisfied the boat would then be in 'patrol routine', which meant we were able to dive safely, once ordered.

When we arrived at the submarine exercise area, which would be beyond the twenty-fathom depth-line, the captain would order a 'diving signal' to be transmitted; this gave our Squadron Operation's Officer our position, and intentions. When he was ready the captain would order the officer of the watch (OOW) to come below and dive the submarine using the klaxon. Responding to this, the OOW would order the bridge cleared of personnel, usually there would only be the lookout, as once in patrol routine those not required to fulfil any function would have departed. The voice-pipe cock would be shut by the lookout as he descended to the control room, which was immediately below the bridge, following just behind him, the OOW would pull the hatch shut, and then press the klaxon's button twice. Peering upward from the control room the lookout would report when the upper hatch was clipped and secure.

The raucous blasts of the klaxon would trigger a flurry of action – the main engines are stopped and shut off from the sea, power to the propellers now coming from the main motors. With the telegraphs set to order 'half ahead, group up', all main vents would be opened at the second klaxon blast and the forward hydroplanes having been turned out in response to the klaxon, would be set to dive. Both the fore, and the after planes-men, would maintain the angle of dive required, before levelling off at whatever depth the captain had ordered. The first lieutenant would endeavour to 'catch a trim'; he wouldn't be satisfied until the boat could maintain the required depth at slow speed, and with minimal use of the hydroplanes. Conserving battery power and silent operation were the objectives, but the requirement of allowing periscope view, without too much of the periscope showing above the surface, might mean temporary speeding-up while trim was adjusted.

The submarine now dived and in good trim, it was usual then to go to 'watch diving', therefore as the crew were divided into three watches, those of whichever watch was scheduled to be on duty, would take over the positions of those whose diving station it was. Unless it was an emergency any subsequent dive would be carried out by using just those actually on watch at the time.

Both the off-duty watches could relax, after whatever other work they might have to do, such as cleaning or maintaining equipment. They knew that as soon as our expected targets were viewed from the periscope, 'action stations' would be ordered. We might be expecting either a lone anti-submarine warship, or perhaps an escorted convoy, depending on the complexity of the exercise required by the training class.

If these trainees were engineering or electrical specialists, more often than not we would have a period of `snorting'. This entailed bringing the boat to periscope depth, raising and then draining the snort mast to enable the oxygen supply to the main diesel engines so they could be used to generate electrical power to replenish the batteries. This could be carried out in a number of ways depending whether the need was for maximum power generation, or if there was a requirement to cover distance while also charging.

Day running suited a newly married such as me, just as it did all those others whose wives and families lived locally, but when certain exercises needed us to be in deeper and more open waters, these would have to be carried out somewhere in the western approaches, off Land's End. For us to be in position, ready for an early start on the Monday, we needed to sail before midnight on Sunday. These exercises would usually carry on until the Friday afternoon, when our canny captain would endeavour for us to be in that part of the exercise area which was furthest east, to be ready for a speedy return to base, as soon as cessation of the exercise was declared by whoever was the senior officer. We found it galling, to see those surface vessels that had left Portsmouth on the Monday a few hours after us, now come steaming past us homeward bound at twenty-five knots, as we struggled along at our best speed of about sixteen knots.

Not with the ease of the crew in mind

For a small vessel, with a crew of only around sixty men a submarine has a diverse mix of specialities, around fifteen in total, each having their own role to fulfil. For me at harbour stations, once the crew had come aboard, I would turn out the fore-planes from their housings and check them in their 'rise' and 'dive' extremities, before returning them to their housed position. I would then shut and secure the torpedo loading hatch. While in harbour, this hatch is used as the prime entry/exit point. The reason: because it is the only angled hatch, and as such it is suitable to fit a stairway-type of ladder to. (The other hatches are all circular, and are fitted with vertical access ladders). The design of the hatch was not with the ease of the crew in mind, but primarily to enable the loading of the twenty-foot long, one and a half ton torpedoes. These would be hoisted aboard by crane from the jetty in a cradle, which would then fit into the track of the loading rails which led through the hatch to the torpedo stowage compartment below. As a matter of routine I would always instruct those working below the hatch not to stand in front of the rails. So often would I tell them that it caused my working party to mimic my words in annoyance, until that time when one of those weighty torpedoes broke loose and came hurtling down through the hatch and ending up with the nose-cone crushed against the steel plating of the bulkhead, in front of which they would have been standing. When fully armed we would have a torpedo in each of the six tubes, and six reload torpedoes, three stowed on each side of the compartment. Each of these torpedoes, could be fitted with either a warhead containing over eight-hundred pounds of Torpex explosive mixture, or they could be fitted with what we knew as a 'blowing- head'; obviously on a war patrol they would all be fitted with the explosive warhead. A torpedo fitted with the blowing-head, had water ballast instead of the explosive mixture; at the end of its run, the ballast would automatically be blown, causing the torpedo to float nose-upwards in the water which would allow recovery of the expensive weapon. While torpedo-loading takes place, the bunks for the eighteen men who sleep in this compartment had to be dismantled.

Once I had secured the hatch to be ready for sea, I fitted strong-backs across the area in which the angle of the hatch had been formed, to replace that part of the strengthening ribs of the hull which had been cut away. These ribs are 18 inches apart throughout the length of the hull. When not in use the torpedo loading rails were secured upwards toward the deck head. Across the rails we would then fit wooden slats to form the stowage for bread and for sacks of vegetables and potatoes. This produce would remain fresh for the first week or so of any voyage, after then our food would be fresh from a tin! The water-tight doors that lead into the tube space are kept shut and clipped when at sea for safety reasons, especially when in the confines of the harbour. Having a relatively small volume it was the only compartment that if it became flooded, meant we could still remain afloat.

Once the order 'open up for diving' was passed, I would remove the main vent cotter pins of no.1 and no.2 ballast tanks and then make sure the compartment was ready for the first lieutenant to inspect.

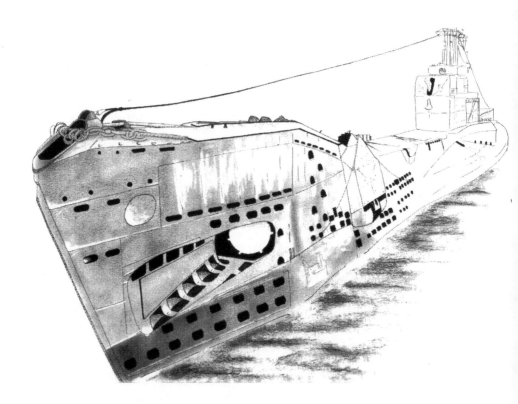

The goddess of fertility and the protector of sailors

It must have been around the end of September 1949 when I travelled north to join Artemis, an A class submarine of the third flotilla whose base was the depot ship HMS Montclare. According to Greek mythology Artemis is 'the goddess of fertility and the protector of sailors', so that seemed a good omen.

The depot ship was moored in Rothesay Bay, Isle of Bute, at the mouth of the River Clyde, which at that time was the operation hub closest to where the cold war surveillance effort was happening. I wasn't happy to be leaving Gosport, as Beryl and I were beginning to furnish and shape our new home, to give it the character that suited us. I also hoped to have the same self-sufficiency with vegetables from the garden as I had enjoyed as a lad, but that would not be easy to achieve with the demands of naval life. Artemis had been in commission for some time, and already had a fully trained and tight-knit crew who were led by an experienced and war-decorated captain. I arrived by boat to board Montclare, and was greeted at her quarterdeck by 'Snowy' Tunman, Artemis's coxswain. He told me that their Jimmy had left him inboard to organise some special equipment required for her forthcoming trip north. He greeted me warmly and said I had been recommended by Dolphin's drafting coxswain as being suitable to replace their previous UW2, who had been posted to work at the escape training-tank. He said that as I was a leading seaman and passed for petty officer, I was entitled to be the `killick-in-charge' of the forward mess. I told Snowy that I would rather not 'upset the applecart', so as long as the present killick is doing a good job, I would rather settle in and get to know the boat as I had not served on an 'A' Class boat and I had a lot to learn. Snowy then said that I would have my work cut out anyway, because the torpedo instructor is temporarily doing duty as second coxswain, therefore I would be in charge in the fore-ends.

I had only brought that amount of kit that would fit into my green leather-edged suitcase, that which had been issued to me to replace the one I had lost on the Prince, but not used until now. I had no intention of lugging a full kit bag to Scotland as I had been told that Artemis was scheduled to carry out snorting trials in the Solent within three months so I could retrieve the remainder of my kit from Dolphin then.

The following morning, Artemis returned from sea to her berth alongside Montclare, and I went aboard at noon just as the rum ration was being issued. That was a good time to meet the other mess-members who were all strangers to me, although I had seen a couple of them as trainees aboard Trespasser. This was not unusual, if you bear in mind that each boat has a small number of crew, and the boats themselves are dispersed to different areas of the world. When serving on a submarine you may work very closely with others of your crew for months, or even for a year or two, and then, for whatever reason, the crew would split asunder at the end of the boats commission and you might never see many, or even any of them, again.

Noticing the medal ribbons sewn on my uniform jacket, the leading signalman told me about our commanding officer, Lieutenant Commander Crawford, whose nickname was

'Tubby', though we wouldn't refer to him as that - well not to his face anyway. Tubby had twice been awarded the Distinguished Service Cross. The first was for his time spent as the first lieutenant of Upholder when it was commanded by Lieutenant M.D. Wanklyn, who was awarded the Victoria Cross for the sinking of the highest tonnage of enemy shipping by any of our submarines. Previous to this, Tubby had been first lieutenant with the legendary submarine commander Ben Bryant. Bryant was credited with the sinking of the most enemy ships. Upholder was sunk with the loss of all aboard her shortly after Tubby had left her to take over the command of Unseen. With him in command, Unseen sank four enemy ships and survived long periods while being depth-charged by enemy escort vessels. It was his submarine that had placed those sonar beacons which guided LSTs such as mine for landings along the coast of North Africa during 1942. During the early summer of 1943, Unseen completed four missions around Sicily, to survey those beaches selected as being most suitable to use as landing areas. His total of twenty-seven war-patrols was a record number, and all were conducted at a time of high submarine losses. Rewarding that leadership and his tenacity during these risky exploits, he was awarded his second DSO.

Looking at the captain you wouldn't describe him as being tubby, except perhaps for his face, and also he was not what you might expect a dynamic, heroic leader in the Hollywood 'make-believe' image to be. I found him to be calm and gentlemanly, always considerate to us more lowly beings, and not at all overbearing.

Mentioning heroes; while in Dolphin, I had been on friendly terms with another highly decorated man, a real heroic individual by the name of James (Jim) Macgennis VC. Jim, a fellow leading seaman had been 'mentioned in despatches', to record his valiant service as the seaman-diver aboard a midget submarine during attacks which disabled the German battleship Tirpitz, while she was supposedly safe from attack in the protected anchorage behind anti-submarine nets, at Kafjord, Norway. Subsequently, in July 1945, during another midget submarine attack, he attached limpet mines to the under-parts of the hull of the Japanese cruiser Takao, while she was at anchor in the Jahore Straits, off Singapore. Jim, whose actions were so risky and extraordinary, was awarded the Victoria Cross.

I often would have a pint or two with Jim, at Dolphin's NAAFI bar, but would not stay for too long, because the rum would start to flow at a vast rate. I admired Jim hugely. He started life growing up around the staunchly catholic Falls Road area of Belfast, and was not really accepted by the protestant majority; and yet he chose to serve the crown, against some opposition, and went on to become forever regarded as one of the greatest of our submariner heroes. I wish he could have been supported better to cope with the fame that came along with the medal. I have no doubt that in today's more enlightened times, he would have been. I was pleased when after fifty-five years had elapsed, he was given full recognition with the unveiling of a memorial to him in the grounds of the City Hall Belfast, unfortunately this happened after Jim had passed away.

Before leaving Rothesay to sail north, two watches were given a 'long weekend' leave. I had been checking flights from Glasgow to Northolt, the then London airport, and knew that within about three hours I could board the Portsmouth-bound train from Waterloo. I can't remember the cost but thought it worth paying to be home for two clear days. I managed to convince an artificer and the radio supervisor of the soundness of doing this, so we travelled together. The news of our mode of travel spread throughout the boat, because it was so unusual to do weekend-return travel by air, for us ordinary folk anyway. The three of us were seasoned sailors, and as such we were used to the often pitching and rolling motion of a ship while at sea, but after suffering the bumpy flight on this plane, a Douglas DC3, we were all 'green about the gills' due to the turbulence. Fortunately, the return flight was smooth and we soon forgot the previous discomfort. Thereafter any chance we had to get home for a weekend, we would travel by air.

Icebergs don't have navigation lights

It became obvious we were heading for a cold place when electrical ratings from Montclare began installing five-bar electric heaters throughout the boat, and when those numerous stores that we needed were loaded, as well as thick, long-sleeved vests, and long-johns for us to wear under our trousers. The amount of tinned food was another indication that our time away from base would be lengthy. As usual, these events were not to be talked about outside of our own crew, not to other submariners, or to the crew of Montclare. One of our killick stokers told us that during last spring his previous boat, Ambush, had carried out snorting trials as far north as the arctic icepack. The snort mast, like the one fitted to this boat only a year ago, allows the submarine to recharge her batteries while submerged by using the diesel engines to generate power. He said that storms they encountered were so violent that to enable sleep they had to lash themselves to their bunks. His experience gave us forewarning of what we could expect.

The best time for optimum light in the Arctic is October and November which is when we would be there. The weather was good until we were north of Bear Island, then the wind backed and came from a north-westerly direction, bringing with it cold winds that had crossed the Arctic ice. Throughout most of this time I had no view of those weather conditions as I had no reason to be on the bridge, even if I had wanted to be there. It was cold enough just being down below inside the boat, even while wearing those thick under-garments. Those electric fires threw out only enough heat to keep some of the ice at bay, while the condensation they had helped to produce formed icicles, which would hang like stalactites from the hull above our heads. When we dived to carry out periods of snorting, the freezing air that those oxygen-hungry diesel engines sucked in through the snort mast would cause ice to form in the usually hot engine room. When on the surface, the diesel engines which were pounding away to keep us forever heading north, to thrust our way through whatever sea-state the north-westerly winds were creating, would be sucking their air supply through the open hatch and the conning-tower that led upwards to the bridge. The air-blast would be laced with ice formed from the sea-spray, making the control room an uncomfortable place to be.

For a change of my routine, I took an opportunity to experience what was happening up top when I elected to relieve the look-out. He was needed to assist the second coxswain in the breaking-up of a thick ice layer which had formed around the periscope standards; those supports which protect the exterior parts of the periscopes and aerials. The dry binoculars I took up with me to the bridge, to use while on look-out, I soon found to be virtually useless. Those waves that came from just off our port bow had long over-hanging crests. As the waves tumbled over, they streamed dense white streaks of foam which blew as a curtain of spray in the wind and caused our field of vision to be very limited. Before I had struggled to climb upwards through the inrushing air to get to the bridge, I had donned a weather-proof outfit, that known as a 'penguin suit'. Although supposedly 'proof', the weather in the form of icy damp would eventually find its way inside. After my use of them, the penguin suit and the binoculars would be left to dry-out in the engine room, to be ready for when another oncoming look-out would use them. There could be little or no conversation with the officer of the watch while I was on the bridge because of the howling fifty-knot wind, and the thump and thud as each thirty-foot wave struck against our fore-casing and threw up another ice-laced curtain of spray that would bite into the facial area the penguin-suit had to leave exposed, to allow use of the almost useless binoculars! Fortunately, risk of collision was minimal as very few vessels were foolhardy enough to venture this far north, except for

those intrepid fishermen who would follow those fish wherever they happened to go.

Soon we would be seeing what are called berg bits or growlers: small parts of icebergs sometimes about three feet in height above the surface. These could cause damage to our periscopes once we had dived. The navigating officer said to me one time "Icebergs don't have navigation lights if we hit one, at whatever speed, it could cause a disaster". (A submarine is kept afloat on the surface by ballast tanks attached to the sides of its pressure hull, the strength of these is just sufficient to withstand limited pressure and bumping when alongside but not by being struck by an iceberg).

Our captain, usually imperturbable, seemed to be quite tense, often checking and re-checking the charts as navigation in these latitudes was difficult. The radar-plot rating, who was also the navigator's yeoman, informed me that some of these Arctic-Ocean charts had not been updated by further surveying since the eighteen hundreds. Also he thought that the underwater topography was uncertain, few sounding lines were shown to indicate what depth might be beneath our keel once we had submerged deep enough to be clear of pack ice. What uncharted rock pinnacles were there was anyone's guess, so it was probably best for our state of mind if we didn't ponder that question.

The little I did know (because the captain would only tell us that which he thought we needed to know, once he thought that we needed to know it) was that at the end of just a two month voyage, the little clothing I had brought with me, and had kept stowed in my two foot by eighteen-inch personal locker and in my new leather-edged suitcase, was damp and becoming mildewed, and the case itself had absorbed too much moisture for it to be of any further use.

Norwegian haircut

The Arctic snorting, that we and other boats were trialling, was experience-building, even for our very experienced captain, this being a first time for him, as well as for most of us. This ability was performance enhancing, and vital for the when our boats would be stationed in areas around the Barents Sea. Those same areas the Soviet's used for naval exercises, and through which their ships and submarines had to transit after leaving their bases for deployment in the Atlantic. We would not be able to snort with impunity, for whenever we were within Russian territorial waters we needed to be wary of our presence being discovered, either by visual sightings, ship-borne radar or by our main adversary, airborne anti-submarine radar. Our passive listening aerial was raised and monitored whenever we snorted, to enable the detection of the aircraft's high frequency transmissions. Any detection, from whatever source, would cause us to stop snorting and go deep, until it was judged to be safe enough for us to resume snorting.

Our other enemy, the weather, was in my experience rarely calm enough to complete the battery charge without having some interruption during a period of snorting. Maintaining depth in rough weather would be difficult and especially so in a following sea. The fore-plane's watch-keeper was 'chasing the bubble', as he tried to keep the bubble of the inclinometer level and the needle of the depth gauge at the ordered depth. That depth, required to keep both the periscope and the snort head just above the surface of the sea, was difficult to achieve in perhaps fifteen-foot waves and virtually impossible in sea states higher. Each time the snort head submerged, its shut-off valve would operate and cause the oxygen-hungry diesel engines to get their air supply from within the boat. This of course would create a vacuum, resulting in our eardrums popping and in need of continual clearing which would make sleep difficult for those who were off-watch. You must bear in mind that we would need to snort for periods of perhaps six hours to replenish our batteries with that power we had used while submerged. If, or when, this vacuum reached what was considered a critical level, the engines would be stopped until such time we could be in that trim necessary to be able to recommence our period of snorting. I haven't mentioned before that during darkness, or in those periods of gloom as experienced in arctic half-light, the control room would be in dim red-lighting. This would enable optimum night vision for those at the periscope when dived, or for those going up to the bridge when on the surface. Blackout curtains would be rigged to shield the control room from that bright lighting required elsewhere on the boat. When we were using the noisy diesel engines it was obviously the best time for the clamour of any vital maintenance and also when we would blow the contents of the sewage tank to sea; at all other times we would preserve an 'ultra-quiet' state.

Maintaining this silent state would be vital, because we might be actively hunted and attacked, as when later in my service I took part in two 'mystery tours' (our name for the clandestine intelligence-gathering missions). Both these times it was in areas to the north of Norway, and when I was serving aboard those submarines known as 'T Conversions'. These boats had been lengthened and streamlined to make them quieter, faster and stealthier. The lengthening was necessary to enable the insertion of another pair of main motors, and extra battery capacity.

For reasons unknown to me, after we had surfaced at the conclusion of these snort trials, we closed with the Norwegian coast and headed through a series of scenic islands to the port of Alesund where we berthed amongst fishing boats alongside a jetty sited close to the town's centre. We, the crew, were quite unprepared for this as none of us had brought with us our No.1 uniform suits which we would use when going ashore. Nonetheless, those of us not on duty smartened up the best we could and headed off into the town, the majority getting no further than the nearest bar. I had other plans, because I knew that as soon as we got back to Rothesay I was going on leave to Gosport. Not wanting to waste any time when doing that I sought out the nearest barber's shop, where my month-old beard could be shaved, and my unkempt hair shorn. The first barber-shop that I came across had two or three customers waiting for their turn in the chair, so I walked along the street until I came to another that had no queue. Fate must have intervened to take me there because the barber, a man in his late fifties, was overjoyed to see a British naval rating in his shop. He told me of the suffering caused by the German occupation, and that members of his family had served with British forces against those of Germany. He then insisted I should go with him to his home after he had cut my hair. Even though it was early in the afternoon he shut up the shop and then drove me to his house on the outskirts of the town. His wife and his two grown-up sons greeted me warmly, and before long their house became crowded with others who were their neighbours and friends, and I became the centre of everyone's attention. They had plated-up a feast of their traditional dishes, such as preserved cod and spiced sausage, along with other cold meats and pickled vegetables, some of which I couldn't identify. I felt some embarrassment when accepting their hospitality with nothing to offer them in return, as I was aware of the hardships they had suffered throughout the Nazi occupation, but they insisted. All the while as we were eating, toasts were proposed to every person around the table and in particular to me, and to Winston Churchill, to their King Haakon and his son Crown Prince Olav and also to Britain's king and queen. We also toasted 'Milorg' (a resistance group which became evident to me that my host had a role within throughout those years of occupation) and we all cursed Hitler and Quisling, and also the Russians, who they regarded as being untrustworthy as neighbours. Not once did they ask anything about my boat or of her movements, but they wanted to hear of my wartime experiences.

After the proposal of each toast, or each curse, the word 'skal' was our signal to down in one gulp the contents of our long-stemmed glass. This glass was full of Akevitt which I assumed they had distilled at home from potatoes. Drinking this it reminded me of my father and the home-brewed wines that we enjoyed together. After each toast we all had to refill our glass from the tap of the big oak cask that we were stood around, and to be ready with a name, for whoever's turn it was next, to either honour or to damn the person of his choice. Whenever it was my turn to propose the toast, I would usually say "To my wonderful wife Beryl". All those present would reply "To your wonderful wife Beryl and may god bless her" in their Norwegian manner.

I don't remember being driven back to the boat but I do remember the whole crowd of them singing their patriotic songs as I unsteadily crossed our gangplank, and some others of our crew joining in as they made their own way back aboard, they with other Norwegians they had met while in the bar. Whenever, since then, that my hair needs a trim my mind drifts back to that time at Alesund, and to those welcoming people.

A New world order

I thought at the time 1950 was the start of a new world order,
but our towns and cities still had many vacant bomb-sites and
unrepaired homes, including those of Portsmouth and
Gosport. The rebuilding would be a slow process as the
nation was spending triple what we do today on defence and
had four times the number of service personnel trying to
maintain a global presence. We emerged from the world war
as one of the 'big three' having the psychology of a victor, but
with the economic circumstances of a defeated nation. Unlike
the Germans and the Japanese who chose to spend the money
they received under `Marshall Aid' rebuilding infrastructure
and industry, we chose to preserve the illusion of being a

world power and squandered our more considerable sums in futile attempts while doing that.

Some of those abandoned military bases from the war had to be reactivated in response to the heating-up of the cold war. As Churchill had feared, the Empire was beginning to unravel and soon would be jettisoned with unseemly haste: India had gained her independence and other countries were seeking theirs.

Slowly things did begin to improve within the economy in the war's aftermath. One indication of this was that the rationing of fuel would be ended this year. This hadn't really affected me (even though by now I was the owner of a motor cycle) because I always safely stored some petrol at home, just in case the local garage had no remaining stock. The motor-bike I had bought was a year-old BSA Golden Flash; the 350cc model, which was the first of their post war production.

The past winter had been a difficult one for Beryl, because the highest paid secretarial position she could find, since moving down to Gosport, was located in Southsea. This entailed for her a bus ride to the ferry, then boarding the often crowded ferry-boat to get to Portsmouth, and after that to endure the four-mile bus journey to Southsea; all this during what had been harsh winter weather. Being a naval wife, and with no family or friends close-by it could be quite lonely for her. Those friends she met while at work lived the other side of the harbour. If we had lived on a married quarter's housing estate (like that under construction then at Rowner in Gosport) there would be other wives whose husbands also might be at sea, so she could have company of those in a similar situation to her. By the time she had returned home after having worked all day, she had little time for any social events outside of our home.

Towards the end of this same year Beryl changed her employment to work as a teaching assistant, and the school she worked at was within walking distance of our home. Beryl already possessed that education requirement needed to become a teacher, so her aim now was to gain experience, and then as soon as we could afford the money, she would embark on a twelve month teacher's training course.

Artemis was scheduled to return to Gosport, from where we were due to conduct snort trials out in the Solent; to test modifications to the snort system and to be filmed by the naval film unit, but before this would happen, at the request of the Manchester City Council we were sent to Manchester to` show the flag'. In order to reach our berth at Trafford Wharf we had to traverse the Manchester ship canal, where at every vantage point we were greeted by cheering sightseers, probably because it was the first time a submarine had done this. It was also a chance for the people of that locality to meet those whose exploits they had heard of during the war (although by this time we had less than a dozen crew-members with any actual war-service). It would also provide an opportunity for those of our crew who lived in the vicinity of Manchester to have their families come aboard.

Artemis had worked her magic with regard to fertility, for in this year the wives of five crew-members had become pregnant. Later in this year Beryl and I would be attending two church christening ceremonies to be held locally at Gosport. We were still young, Beryl 22 and me 26, so we planned to get our house in order, metaphorically speaking, before we started a family of our own.

It wasn't until July 1971, long after I had left the submarine service and in the twilight of Artemis's own service, the protector of sailors was called upon in her guardian role. By an inexcusable mishap or poor submarine practice, call it what you will, the boat was sunk alongside the jetty at HMS Dolphin. Most of those crew-members who were on-duty aboard her, managed to get ashore to safety, but the three who weren't able to shut themselves in the forward escape compartment. The boat had sunk 35ft to the bottom of the creek. When eventually it was declared safe to carry out the escape procedure, the three men rose to the surface in what was a textbook free ascent. Artemis's work was done, and after she was raised to the surface it was decided because of extensive saltwater damage, and her limited remaining lifespan (being now 25 years old) she would be scrapped.

This year 4,000 British soldiers would be sent to Korea as part of the Commonwealth Brigade, where they, along with other United Nations troops would assist those of the US and of South Korea, to halt the advance into the south of the Soviet backed North Korean and Chinese armies. Among those British troops were soldiers from the Gloucestershire Regiment, some of whom were known to Beryl and her family, and a few were also known to me. The bloodiest day of that war, which claimed the lives of more of our men than did the Falklands conflict, both the Iraq wars, and that in Afghanistan combined, was in April 1951. This, the most desperate action fought by the British Army since world war two, was known as the battle of the Imjin River. During this battle those 750 men of the 1st Battalion, 'The Glorious Glosters', were ordered to hold a part of the line of advance of the Chinese brigades, estimated to have been around 27,000 in number. After much heroic fighting, much of it at close quarters, 620 of the battalion were either killed, captured or taken as prisoners-of- war.

It was the unenviable duty of Beryl's father, as a policeman, to convey the sad news to the families of some of those who had been killed or taken prisoner.

A lucky break

Crossing the Chesil beach I could open the throttle and get the bike into top gear. I had ridden down the hill from HMS Osprey and through the town of Fortuneswell with the care it deserved, and now was happy to speed away. The course at Osprey now complete, I could now sew my UW1 (under water weapons, first class) badges to the sleeves of my uniform shirts and jackets to replace those badges that depicted a UW2 (second class). I had already changed those of my working dress jacket, working shirts and my overalls: the clothing that I will wear on Monday, when I join the submarine Affray as her petty officer, torpedo instructor. My role aboard her will be to be in charge of her fore-end, the torpedoes and their launching tubes. I would have around half a dozen men to supervise in this work. I had been told that we will have a Royal Marine's SBS detachment aboard, which meant that their two fol-boats (a type of folding canoe) will have to be stowed in the fore-end until the time came to launch them. I had helped carry out this operation while on other submarines. It was always a nuisance to us as these boats occupied that same space that we used while working on the torpedoes, which we regarded as our bread and butter, our purpose in life if you will. Like most other submariners, I would have no wish to swap places with those intrepid marines and preferred to admire them from a distance.

Riding back to Gosport I would take the A352, the coastal route, which after leaving Weymouth would take us through Wool to Wareham. Then by following the A35 we would pass through Poole, Bournemouth and Christchurch. After passing through Mudeford I could open the throttle and zip through the New Forest, whilst keeping an eye out for those ponies that would graze by the verge, as they sometimes would cross the road in front of vehicles; also, I tried to watch out for the difficult-to-avoid deer, they could appear from behind shrubbery very suddenly. Those animals could spoil any motor-bike ride. Slowing the bike down as I rode through Lyndhurst, I was pleased that as I had expected, it being early April, the town was traffic free. Free from the caravan-towing cars which used this holiday route during the summer season: a route that I would then avoid.

My new BSA Golden Flash was a 650cc twin A10 model. Its engine seemed to purr along and had more responsive power than my former bike, a 350cc model. I changed to the more powerful bike as we could hitch a side-car to it without losing performance whenever we carried a passenger, or if Beryl needed to be more suitably dressed for any formal occasion. Passing through Southampton I joined the A27 at Woolston, knowing that in about 35 minutes I would be at home with Beryl for the weekend. My pillion passenger, chief torpedo instructor Les Knowles, was dressed in his long great-coat, the pockets of which were stuffed with fresh farm eggs, each single egg wrapped in newspaper. He was pretty good as a pillion passenger but not like Beryl – she would be with me like glue as we rounded bends or weaved through traffic: the epitome of the ideal pillion rider. I would be at sea Monday morning aboard Affray and Les would be back at his desk at HMS Dolphin. I was glad of my warm clothing, my pilot's leather flying-helmet with its fleece lining and the air-crew flying suit that I wore whenever the air was chilly. (Many of us wore no motor cycle helmet or purpose designed motor-bike leathers in those days). Those clothes kept me warm and more importantly were keeping me dry as we rode through a seasonal rain shower. I was taking particular care this day because it was Friday the 13th and we in the navy are somewhat superstitious about that date. Riding downhill at Bursledon I steered out into the centre of the road to pass a bus, stationary at a bus-stop; what I wasn't able see was that the bus driver had beckoned the driver of a Bedford people-carrier to come out from the side-road on the left. At the last moment I saw it emerge from in front of the bus and, instinctively, I applied the brakes. This braking caused the bike to slew to the left which pitched me forwards. I skidded underneath the Bedford and became wedged between the road and its exhaust pipe. I must have been stunned by the impact; the next thing I remember was its driver calling out to me to find out if I was alright. I said "I will be if you turn off the ******* engine: its exhausts fumes are choking me! Les had skidded across the road to the far pavement. He was shaken but unhurt, and with others he helped me to get out from under the vehicle. I was suffering pain from the area around my left arm and shoulder, so it wasn't long before I was in the ambulance that had been summoned and on my way to Southampton hospital. The X-rays they took showed that my left humorous bone was broken, so my arm was protected with plaster and supported with a sling. Because I had been stunned they kept me in the hospital overnight. When Les came to visit me the next morning he told me that as my bike was only slightly damaged it had been recovered and taken to my home. He was very pleased to report that none of his eggs were either cracked or broken!

For me, with ten years of accident-free riding, this was my one and only spill. Once again luck was on my side, a very lucky break you might say! Affray sailed on Monday 16th April 1951, taking someone else in my place. After diving in her ordered position, which was south of the Isle of Wight, she was fated never to come back up to the surface. Seventy-five men died, in circumstances which have not been fully investigated. Amongst them was the man who took my place, those friends I had visited two weeks before she sailed (to let them know I would be joining them on completion of my course) and their experienced war-decorated captain, whose former home I see most days as it is very close to my own home.

On the Esplanade at Gosport's harbour-front, overlooking the jetty of HMS Dolphin from where she sailed - a memorial to Affray has been erected. It names those seventy-five men who perished in such awful circumstances. I was at the dedication service for the memorial, which was unveiled by the widow of a crew-member, she voiced what many of us were thinking at that time "I feel that they have been done justice at last, it's been sixty-two years, too long a time"

Ignorance is bliss

While recovering from my broken arm I was placed on light duties at HMS Vernon. It was in their sick bay that the Surgeon Lieutenant removed my plaster of Paris dressing to check my arm's movement, after some probing and wiggling, he said, "Sorry, I think I have broken the bone again". That meant for me another six weeks of light duties, spent doing meaningless tasks; and all that time the sonar hunt for Affray was happening, until after six weeks of searching, they found her. Like many others in the submarine community (and elsewhere) I was hoping that she, the submarine, and they, the crew, could be recovered and brought back home.

When I was declared 'fit for duty' I joined the submarine Tactician on a temporary basis, shortly before her deployment to Arctic waters; once again I was heading to the north of Norway. It was with some trepidation we learnt from the captain that we would be venturing under the ice-cap. Those not on-watch had been mustered in the fore-ends to hear his address. When he said that navigation under the ice would be difficult, as we would just rely on 'dead reckoning', or guess work as the cynic might say, nobody said a word – we just looked at each other in silence. You can imagine it was with some relief, when, after a few hours under ice, we surfaced and found ourselves to be safely back in clear water. You have to realise that only those of the crew actually on watch in the control room would have any idea of what was going on, or know what depth the boat is at, and I was one of those left in complete ignorance. It is often said that ignorance is bliss, but often 'imaginings' are worse than knowing the facts!

I know of several other of these under-ice forays carried out by conventional submarines; Finwhale, in 1963, broke through Arctic ice with her strengthened fin, after having detected a suitable thin patch with her upward-pointing underwater cameras. Then, in 1965 she travelled 95 miles, again while under Arctic ice. A member of my local 'submariners association' branch has shown me photos taken of Grampus on the surface after having broken through thin ice. One photo, taken in March 1963, shows crew-members playing a game of football on the surrounding ice-cap, they recorded the temperature as being 23 degrees below zero.

My next posting was to another 'T' Class: this time it was the recently streamlined Tireless. This streamlining was done to enable her to have more speed and it was achieved by removal of her external torpedo tubes and the gun to reduce drag through the water. With this smoothing-out of water-flow it also helped to reduce that noise detectable by anti-submarine search sonar.

Tireless was soon to be on her way north, not to the Arctic but to Scotland, and more specifically to the Arrochar torpedo range, sited at the head of Loch Long which is a spur off the River Clyde. The purpose of this deployment was to carry out development trials on the prototype Mark 12 torpedo, known as the Fancy. I would not be involved with this, because I would be watch-keeping in the control-room. My duties would be split during each three-hour watch between operating the forward hydroplanes to keep the ordered depth, at the steering position, and with operating the engine and main motor telegraphs, as required, while recording times of changes to course, depth, and motor or engine speeds in the control room log book.

The Fancy's propulsion unit was fuelled by HTP (high-test peroxide) and not the usual diesel. This unit is housed in the same casing as that used on the standard Mark 8 torpedo, but there the similarity ends; HTP is a volatile fuel and great care must be taken to avoid any contamination to it. The handling and loading of these torpedoes would be carried out by the trials staff, headed by a Lieutenant Commander, and not by our own torpedo-men.

Usually during an attack on a surface or submarine target, torpedoes are fired in an angled spread, to fan out and maximise the chance of one or more strikes on the target, and to counter any alteration of speed or course the target might make after the final firing-calculation has been made. During these trials each Fancy would be fired singly to enable evaluation of its performance.

When these trials were completed to the satisfaction of the trials staff, we headed to the naval facility at Invergordon, on Scotland's east coast, from where we would carry out deep-water trials; firing the Fancy while submerged at greater depths than we could when in Loch Long.

The results of trials, such as these, are made known only to those who need to know, so it was no surprise, to us the crew-members, that we heard no more of the Fancy after we had returned to Gosport.

It was during my leave period when Beryl and I decided, that now we had started a family, we needed to purchase a car. This would be more practical than the motor-bike and side-car when our whole family would travel. During that era the slogan 'British, is Best' encouraged us to buy home produced goods. As I couldn't fault my BSA Golden Flash, and by now I owned a 12' dinghy powered by a very reliable British Seagull outboard motor, and, having read of the virtues of MG's Magnette ZA (first released for sale in October 1953), I was amazed to find that the first motor dealer we visited had exactly that model which he had taken in part-exchange that day. The car's previous owner, a police superintendent from Dorchester, was there and was completing the documentation for his new purchase with the dealer. As it was now February 1955, the car was barely 18 months old and was painted in our desired colour - British Racing Green. Although it was priced above what we had thought of spending, we bought the car there and then, before it was advertised for sale. A wise decision, we owned that car for twenty-five almost trouble-free years, and it probably saved us thousands of pounds in the long term. A couple of years after that, when Beryl needed to have a car to travel daily to the Siskin School (where she worked as a teacher) and being pleased with the MG's reliability she chose to buy a MGB sports model, which she then owned for twenty-three years.

I was on summer leave at the time of my thirty-first birthday, 8th June 1955, and returned to the boat on the 16th just as news was coming in about a horrific occurrence aboard the submarine Sidon, which was alongside the depot ship Maidstone at Portland in Dorset. The following day, more details began to unfold about the disastrous explosion of the HTP propulsion unit of one, of the two, Fancy torpedoes which were loaded in her torpedo tubes. The blast ruptured the front door of the tube which allowed the sea to flood into the forward two compartments, and caused fire, toxic gas and fumes. So violent was the explosion, even though the torpedo wasn't fitted with a warhead, the torpedo-tube rear door hurtled through the accommodation-compartment. Among those thirteen fatalities, and the seven others who were seriously injured, were members of the trials team who were known to us on Tireless, including the Lieutenant Commander.

Sidon, with 56 men aboard, was about to sail in order to test-fire the Fancy torpedoes. If those torpedoes had had their warheads fitted to them, their probable detonation would have made the tragedy even worse. All those aboard still alive managed to escape, some with the brave assistance of a rescue party from Maidstone. One member of that rescue party, who lost his own life while rescuing others, was Surgeon Lieutenant Rhodes of HMS Maidstone. He was posthumously awarded the Albert Medal for 'selfless, brave actions'. Most of the dead are buried at the Royal Naval Cemetery, which overlooks the harbour at Portland. Years later, I attended a ceremony when the memorial to them was unveiled on Portland Bill. A further Fancy propulsion-unit explosion happened during testing at Arrochar which led to the abandonment of the project in 1958.

Two experimental HTP-fuelled submarines, Explorer and Excalibur had recently been launched and were commissioned in 1956. They were built to evaluate German technology for air independent propulsion, as fitted to the XV11 class of U-boat, which were produced at the end of the war. I had seen both of those boats when serving at our base at Faslane; not alongside the depot ship Adamant where the conventional boats berthed, but kept apart from us for safety, alongside their own mother-ship Kingfisher. They soon became known as Exploder and Excruciator because of mishaps with the volatile HTP fuel. Flames had been reported on top of their combustion chambers in the engine- room (which was unmanned for safety while the boat was underway), and on another occasion Explorer's crew had to evacuate the boat onto the casing, to escape a cloud of smoke and fumes which had filled boat's interior, with luck they were on the surface at the time! A reassurance for the crew-members was that both boats were fitted with the latest escape technology! These boats could reach an underwater speed of 25 knots, and were useful to act as high speed targets for our anti-submarine warships, but with the advent of nuclear-powered submarines, and the fact that this technology was not proven safe, both boats were scrapped in 1965.

I thought I had heard the last of HTP torpedoes aboard naval vessels until when, in August 2000, the Russian nuclear submarine Kursk was lost with all 118 crew. This was a result of a fire in an HTP torpedo fitted with a warhead, which then exploded and caused further detonations of all her six other torpedoes. The full story is too long and involved to recount here.

'Q'

Get us down quick tank

My first posting after leaving the Submarine Service and having spent two weeks in the barracks, was to the Devonport-based Daring class destroyer HMS Decoy a unit of the Fifth Destroyer Squadron. In size, she was almost equivalent to the light cruiser Danae, on which I had served what now seems a lifetime ago. The Daring class were the last destroyers to have guns as their main armament; those built after would have guided missiles. These guns were the six, 4.5" quick-firing guns, in three twin turrets, as main armament; along with three, twin 40mm Bofors for close range anti-aircraft defence. Together, these guns could simultaneously engage two targets at long range, and two others at short range, while under full radar-directed control.

My main personal responsibility would be training those who manned the twin torpedo-launching tubes, and also those who operated the Squid anti-submarine mortars which were mounted aft at the quarter-deck; from where they were able to fire over and ahead of the ship.

Being some 200 miles in distance to Gosport it involved quite a lengthy journey to travel home, which is why I had kept the motorcycle as well as having the car. I took any opportunity that arose to get home to see Beryl and our son Nicholas, knowing he would grow up fast and I didn't want to miss too much during his early years. Now that Beryl's father had retired from the police, her parents were looking to move to Gosport so they could live close by and be of help in supporting her so she could maintain her teaching career. They eventually moved into the one of the tower-blocks on Gosport's esplanade. This apartment block has views across to old Portsmouth and to the dockyard, as well as overlooking the interesting harbour and the approaches to it, which are busy at all times with craft of many types.

Decoy was soon involved in a NATO exercise employed as part of a protective screen, guarding RFA supply ships from attacks by our submarines which were in the guise of those of the soviets.

It was a strange feeling for me, now being on the 'other side', as I knew exactly what would be happening aboard those boats below the surface when we on the Decoy steamed in to attack, dropping small explosive charges above where we thought the submarine to be to simulate our squid weapon's firing. I knew how loud these charges would sound to those on the other end of our attack, and how frightening the thump, thump, thumping, of our propeller noise as we crossed above them. They would have flooded their Q 'get-us-down-quick' tank, to ensure they were deep enough to avoid the crushing impact of our sharp bow, as we rushed in to deliver our attack. I could visualise the submarine's captain checking his stopwatch; he knew that in just one minute we, at 30 knots, would travel 1,000 yards and he would be estimating when it was safe for him to return to periscope depth, and hopefully be inside our protective screen to continue his attack. In 1960, Thule one of these submarines which were opposing us today, returned to periscope depth too early and was struck by the Rover class replenishment tanker Brown Ranger. She was lucky to survive without casualties, but due to extensive damage she was scrapped. That return to periscope depth from being deep can be difficult to judge. The merging of many ship's propeller noise in confined waters renders sonar interpretation almost impossible. I have no record of what fate befell her CO, but I do know that his signal to Brown Ranger caused some amusement; it read 'Thules rush in where Rangers fear to tread'. If we fast forward almost sixty years to July 2016, the 'state of the art' nuclear submarine HMS Ambush surfaced below a merchant ship off Gibraltar at 1330hrs on a clear fine day. She is described as having 'world leading sensors to detect submarines and surface vessels' (compared to that primitive and less discerning sonar as fitted to Thule) which proves that these incidents will probably continue to happen.

From the stern of Decoy, I would look out for the smoke candle which should soon bob up to the surface to signify the submarines presence and confirm our attack. So many times before, it had been I who was firing those smoke candles from the submarine's submerged signal injector.

I found Decoy to be a happy ship and not as rigid as some others in the post-war Navy. The main reason for this, I believe, was because her CO was a decorated and 'hands on' war veteran, Captain R H Maurice DSO DSC. The day to day routine was handled by the ship's First Lieutenant, Lieutenant Commander L.W.H. Housan-Taylor. Although an easy going character, he tolerated no nonsense and could be quite impatient, as I was soon to find out.

This exercise culminated with both submarines firing a spread of torpedoes during their final attack on the convoy. These torpedoes, fitted with practice 'blowing-heads' instead of explosive warheads, would be set to run at such depth as were required to pass below the target ships; then, at the end of their 5,000-yard run, the blowing mechanism would activate and the torpedo would bob to the surface and would float nose upwards in the sea. Decoy, being based the closest in distance to where this exercise terminated, was tasked to recover these torpedoes, and it fell to me as the TASI to accomplish this. The blowing-heads, being painted 'dayglo' orange colour, were easy to spot in the water, but they were spread out over a couple of miles. The motor-boat and the whaler, each carrying two experienced torpedo-men tasked to achieve the recovery, were sent off to collect two that were the furthest away, while our ship manoeuvred to be alongside the nearest of the floating torpedoes, so we could pass a line under it and bring it up to the horizontal position. This then enabled us to hoist it inboard for secure stowage on deck.

Having chosen those who I felt were the best men for each part of this whole operation, I became somewhat irate to hear the Jimmy, in his impatience to get the task completed quicker than we were, shouting out instructions from the bridge. It seems he thought that men should get into the sea to pass lines underneath some of the torpedoes, when we had trouble in doing so from above. I was as eager as any to get back to Guzz, from where I could mount my motor-bike and head home to Gosport, but I had no intention of proceeding in any way, other than how we were doing it. He couldn't have held it against me, because on my annual report he stated 'Recommended for advancement to Special Duties Officer'.

Goodwill at Leningrad

Soon after we arrived back at Devonport it was announced that we would be taking part in a 'goodwill' visit to the ports of Copenhagen and Stockholm; and then we would visit Russia's second city, Leningrad. Our visit would coincide with the reciprocal visit to Portsmouth by two of their cruisers Sverdlov and Suvorov, along with their escorting destroyers of the Scory class. We would be an escort to the aircraft-carrier Triumph, flagship of the Commander-in-Chief (C-in-C) Home Fleet, Admiral Sir Michael Denny. The other ships of the escort were another of the Daring class: Diana, two `C' class destroyers, Chieftain and Chevron, as well the fast minelayer Apollo.

Unknown to us at this time, while their ships were in Portsmouth an intelligence-gathering operation was carried out by the diver, Commander 'Buster' Crabbe OBE GM RN, who was clandestinely working for naval intelligence and for the CIA. He inspected underneath the hull of the cruiser Sverdlov in order to ascertain the reason for her excellent manoeuvrability; apparently he discovered an innovative bow-thrust propeller, which could be lowered down a tube set in the hull. Although to my knowledge none of our ships were fitted with anything so evolutionary, I wonder if they might have done something similar while we were in Leningrad.

Known to me was that I had not long ago spent six weeks off of Russia's north coast, aboard one of our submarines that was gathering intelligence of their capabilities, and of their naval movements. It seemed surreal to me when our squadron was met by the Soviet destroyer Odyaronny, to welcome us and to lead us into harbour, and when she fired a 17-gun salute to honour our C-in-C. Triumph later exchanged a national 21-gun salute with a battery on Kotlin Island as we steamed past the breakwaters of Kronstadt harbour, home of the 'Red Banner' Baltic Fleet. Ten miles further on, she then entered the narrow Morskoy canal leading to Leningrad's commercial harbour. At that time Triumph was the largest ship ever to do that: HMS Albion had been the first choice of carrier to send on this trip, but her draught was too great, as the channel was then only dredged to a maximum of 27'. If anything was lost by not sending that modern operational carrier, it was more than made up for by sending Triumph in her role as a cadet training ship. While Triumph was proceeding to her moorings, the remainder of us anchored in the outer harbour. It has been said that those crowds that lined both banks of the River Neva, and who watched from the Schmidt Bridge, were the largest to have greeted any British man-of-war, anywhere in the world. We remained there at anchor until during the middle-watch, because our moorings were beyond the Schmidt Bridge, which to prevent disruption to traffic, could only be opened after midnight to allow us through. After midnight had passed our ships, in turn, weighed anchor and proceeded to their respective buoys beyond the bridge. We awoke to find ourselves in the heart of one of the world's most beautiful cities, and in front of those wonderful buildings that were built during the time of Peter the Great and of the Tzars who ruled Russia after him.

For the whole of our stay our ships were the centre of attraction for curious crowds who peered at us from every possible vantage point, day and night. We had to be at our smartest at all times whenever on deck, and each day, the morning 'colours', and evening 'sunset' ceremonies were performed complete with marine bugler. Our ships would be floodlit after sunset, adding atmosphere to an already beautiful scene.

Leningrad is known for its industrialisation, westernisation and revolution, and did not have the look of a city which had been under siege for over two years between 1941 and 1944. The German troops who encircled the city had tried to starve and bombard them into submission, but their defence was resolute. Over a million lives had been lost, many dying of hunger and others from the cold. When oil and coal supplies ran out, there was no heating. Bodies could not be buried in the frozen earth, and every animal - dogs, cats, rats, and even the birds were eaten to prevent their starvation. The city had been largely rebuilt, especially their national monuments but there remained many damaged buildings. We were taken by coach to visit the Summer Palace and the Siege Museum.

We were supposed to go ashore in groups of at least four, but on one occasion I became separated, and found myself alone and surrounded by a group of young female students. They plied me with questions, curious to know about our Queen, curious also about how we lived at home, and they were amazed that I owned a house of my own and that I didn't have to share it with other families. From their studies they knew of Shakespeare, and of Dickens, and they seemed to think that we in England still lived as people did in those days.

I showed them a photograph of Beryl holding our baby son Nicholas. I told them he was named after Nicholas the wonderworker, the protector of children and sailors, the basis for Santa Claus. I told them that because their first thought was that he was named after Nicholas the Second, who was the last Emperor of Russia (until ultimately being murdered by Lenin's Bolsheviks during the revolution).

The final day of our visit, the weather worsened, and owing to high winds we were unable to sail after midnight; therefore the Schmidt Bridge had to be opened after the morning traffic-rush to allow our departure. This did allow thousands of those very friendly, warm-hearted people to wave us farewell from what had been a memorable visit.

Margaret Thatcher slept here... But not with me!

HMS Vigilant, built as a V class Destroyer in 1943, had served in the Indian Ocean and was involved in the Battle of the Malacca Straits (this was around the same time I served there on Danae). After the war's end, she was converted to be a Type 15, fast anti-submarine frigate, but in 1955 she was further converted to be able to accommodate a training class. When I joined her in 1958, she was the lead ship of the Dartmouth training squadron. My role, when at sea, was to instruct the officer-trainees in anti-submarine warfare, but when in harbour, I would teach them to handle the ships motor-boats. Her commanding officer (CO), Captain Morgan Morgan-Giles DSO, OBE, GM, DL, was also a torpedo and anti-submarine specialist. He was a tall, well-built jovial man, pleasant looking but with a scarred chin, scarred I think during the last of the three plane crashes he was involved in, when he was attached as an advisor to a Wellington bomber squadron which was undergoing training to convert to a torpedo-attack role. The last of those crashes was so serious that he, the only survivor, was lucky to have walked away from it. He suffered only some relatively minor facial injuries

During the war, on four occasions, he had been 'mentioned in despatches'. In 1941 he was awarded the George Medal for 'gallantry and undaunted devotion to duty' during bomb and mine disposal work in Egypt (on one occasion, during the siege of Tobruk, he actually 'swam' a mine out of harbour). Later in the war he ran arms from Italy to Tito's partisans in the Dalmatian Islands and the Yugoslavian mainland, he was awarded the DSO 'for courage, outstanding leadership and devotion to duty', notably for his leadership of an attack on the Croatian island of Lussino.

I didn't realise back then, that I would come to know him and his wife and family quite well. He handed over command of the training squadron in 1959 to be the CO of HMS Vernon the torpedo and anti-submarine base at Portsmouth, and at about the same time I was posted there too.

Soon after I arrived at Vernon, I was called to the regulating office and asked if I would like to become the new captain's boat-coxswain, and also his personal driver. I don't know if the CO had input into that request, or whether it was solely a regulating office decision; they were obviously aware I was a car driver as it was they who issued the car permits. (They didn't have many permits to issue as only half a dozen or so at any one time on the base were car owners). Quite often, as I approached Vernon's main gate either on entering or when leaving the establishment, the quartermaster would salute and wave me through, whether I was driving my own car or one belonging to the captain. I have no doubt that only happened because it was rare for anyone, other than a senior officer, to be driving a car. (This was of course, before those times of IRA or other terrorism when security was more relaxed. The main concern seemed to be 'were men complying with the dress code' or 'were they smuggling out a few extra, of the issued, cigarettes'.

Whoever it was that nominated me for the position, I jumped at the chance, because I loved both cars and motor boats.

The captain owned five cars, all classic models which he kept at his country house at Wonersh, a hamlet on the outskirts of Guildford. It was from there I would collect whichever car suited his requirement for that day. He might ask me to bring the Rolls or the Bentley, or perhaps the Sunbeam. He also owned a stretched Ford limousine which he usually chose to use whenever he wanted his whole family to come down to Portsmouth. They loved going across to the Isle of Wight where they would have a picnic at a quiet beach. It would be me, and a crew of two others, who would sail his private yacht, but sometimes on a not so pleasant day with a squally wind, we would use the captain's fast motor-boat. His wife, Pamela, would sometimes bring all six of their children, at other times it would be only those not at school. They were aged from 12 years down to a 1 year old; four girls and two boys. She was Australian-born and a wealthy woman in her own right, having received a substantial inheritance. She was known for saying, "A sailor might have a girl in every port, and in my husband's case I am that girl". She would invariably be on the jetty and waiting to greet him, at whichever port his ship happened to visit.

There was little about boats that Morgan-Giles didn't know, having grown up at his father's boatyard and owned boats himself from a young age. Yet despite all his knowledge and experience, he never interfered with any decision I made as his boat coxswain; he only suggested what he thought we should do. One day he asked me to take the boat into a rocky cove on the Isle of Wight's south coast, but I wasn't happy to do so and I refused. He didn't argue but looked a little surprised, but then I took the boat further along the coast, and put into a more hospitable looking place. The next day he said to me "You were quite right about that cove Peacey, bit of a dangerous place with the children aboard".

It was the most enjoyable job I had while in the Navy but unfortunately it didn't last as long as I hoped it would, Morgan-Giles was posted away early in 1961 to become captain of the heavy cruiser HMS Belfast. The next captain of Vernon did not enjoy as much personal wealth as did Morgan-Giles, so obviously had no need of a personal driver or boat-coxswain. He would rely on a car and its driver from the service motor-pool. Morgan-Giles was later knighted and promoted, becoming Rear Admiral, Sir Morgan-Giles. He later chose to retire from the Navy to stand as the Conservative Party parliamentary candidate for Winchester. He was duly elected in 1964. When, in 1971, he heard that his beloved last command HMS Belfast was to be scrapped, he started 'Operation Sea Horse' with the objective of forming a trust to preserve Belfast as a museum. It is in a great part due to his vision and driving energy that the ship is now an important part of the Imperial War Museum. The next time I saw him was some twenty years later, it was when I took my little 16ft motor-cruiser Red Reef alongside his elegant motor yacht Melita (named after the one of his daughters) at his boat's Hamble River moorings, at Swanwick, Southampton. He greeted me in his usual hearty way and invited me aboard Melita to chat about old times and to sample some of his fine Port wine. Morgan-Giles stirred his sleeping cat which stretched, yawned and then moved aside to allow me to sit on the cushioned bunk in the yacht's spacious cabin, just below a sign which stated, 'Margaret Thatcher slept here...but not with me!'

As we sampled his Port wine, we toasted Maggie Thatcher for those rebates she had wrested back for us by wielding her handbag, from the EU. She was no pussycat, and apart from Churchill who we compared her with as a war leader, neither of us could name a politician who would have embarked on that operation to retake the Falkland Islands, and seen it through to completion. I wondered how soundly she had slept on this very bunk or did her mind drift back to those fateful decisions she had taken. Both of us knew from our own experience that those stored away memories especially of horrific incidents do play on the mind, and sometimes affect how one relates to those around them, especially those who you would not want to hurt. To lighten the mood Morgan-Giles told me that Maggie had supported his campaign to get better pay equality for the Wrens. I reminded him that his recent speech to Parliament would not be viewed as being politically correct outside of it. While trying to get an increase to the payment of three pence extra per day after a Wren's four years of service, he said, "That's not much to give a girl for saying 'Yes sir' all day, and then `No sir' all night." Yet he opposed Wrens serving aboard warships, saying that 'women's eternal role is to create life and nurture it, a fighting man must be prepared to kill. Vive la difference!'

Up close, and smelling the perfume

For me the Cold War was over, but another war was about to heat up when I was posted to be in charge of the main gate at the Duchess of Kent barracks, home of the WRNS (the Wrens) of the Portsmouth command.

Most men of my era, and certainly those in the Navy itself had been in a man's world, even to the extent that happenings at home with one's own wife and family were kept very much separate from service life. Things would gradually begin to change for the better in that respect. I didn't realise back then that I would be on the threshold of this change as, within the Navy and elsewhere in the outside world, the relatively untapped skills and potential of our female colleagues were in great demand.

I knew it would bring challenges for us, the men of the 'dinosaur era', once we got up close and could smell the perfume. From my office at the gatehouse I came to realise the demands on the Wrens, as daily they would head off, in all directions, to where their individual specialisations were required: to Vernon and to Excellent and to those many other establishments situated here in Portsmouth, and across the harbour, to Dolphin, Sultan and Collingwood. It seemed to me even back then that change would need to come about, as recruiting enough men with the skill and aptitude to fill these demanding roles, even just to man the ships, was becoming ever more difficult.

I worked a shift system, week about. During the early shift I would have to ensure that transport was in place and ready to convey them to these locations; on the late shift after they had returned to barracks, like most girls elsewhere in the wider world, they would be glamorizing to spend the evening out there in the Portsmouth nightlife, such as it was in those more austere times. I would need to employ those man-management skills I had acquired when sorting out disputes between men on the mess-deck of a man-o-war, when later they returned, to be back in barracks at their allotted time, which I think was 22.30 hours on weekday evenings. These skills of mine were a bit lacking on the emotional side when sometimes they wanted a father figure to unburden to, but being a father myself, albeit to two not yet in their teens, I would do my best. Realising that it's a fine line to tread, I would always ensure one of the very competent and no-nonsense leading wrens was on hand to back me up. I did have to be pretty firm with some of the more persistent lads the girls would be saying goodnight to outside of the gate, and would occasionally have to de-escalate situations to avoid them getting out of proportion, because I knew that come the sober, cold light of day, such situations would usually resolve themselves.

One February morning an unexpected phone call from the drafting chief in the barracks, announced, "You are off to Scarborough chief." Not wishing to sound disappointed to be leaving this, a posting close to my home and thinking that this would be something connected to fishery protection duties, I said "That's good it's nice up there." "No Chief, not Scarborough in Yorkshire, you're joining a Type-12 Frigate just out of refit over in the dockyard; she's commissioning in April."

I was surprised to find out that I would be going back to Devon again to be an officer cadet instructor aboard Scarborough, where she was to be lead ship of the Dartmouth training squadron. The other ships were Tenby (which I served aboard at times) and Torquay both also ships of the

Whitby class. Why 'surprised to be selected' in this role again? Well it was because when there before, I was forever being roasted by Officers-in-Charge of training classes. Roasted, because often I would 'spin a yarn', a Jack Tar ditty, to the cadets rather than sometimes be trying to give comprehensive answers to big questions; unfortunately, some of these yarns would be written verbatim in the journals those cadets had to keep - hence the roasting! That story within the yarn could often sum up, and be more memorable, than could a thousand words of rules and regulations as quoted in the seamanship manual. Now and again, I would ask them to bring their journals to me, and I would dictate things for them to write. My wife, a skilled teacher, taught me that if students wrote things down wrongly in that first instance, it was often how they would remember them, and I knew that knowledge is power that is only worthwhile if it is disseminated to those who need to know.

The Squadron CO was Captain Christopher Wake-Walker. It was his father Rear Admiral Frederic Wake-Walker who had 'saved my bacon' all those years ago after the Prince had been damaged by Bismarck. It was his decision not to endanger our ship needlessly by continuing to engage Bismarck, once Hood had been sunk and command of the remaining ships had passed to him. It would have been like sending lambs to the slaughter. This wise decision probably allowed me and many others to live and to fight another day, but it was a decision that would probably have resulted in his court martial without him having had the firm support of Admiral Tovey, C-in-C of the Home Fleet. By another coincidence it was he, that later when Third Sea Lord, had the responsibility to amass the fleet of landing vessels to enable all of those amphibious landings that I was involved with.

This final year of my service was varied and interesting as these ships would take the cadets to ports the Navy would not normally visit so it turned out to be a pleasant way to wind down, while all the time wondering where next my life would take me. This peacetime role was less frantic and gave me the chance to review my career and to wonder if I could have achieved more. I had twice been recommended to undergo officer-training but had decided this was not for me. I knew others of my peer group who had taken this route: some had climbed to quite lofty heights. I had felt disgruntled at times when I knew of others of my then petty officer ranking, some of whom had languished for long periods in barracks or training bases – places where they could catch the eye of those who dealt with promotions, and lo and behold, before too long they would be wearing the 'buttons' of a chief petty officer, while I and others more senior in service, seemed to be overlooked. Of course it's not good for the soul to dwell on the unfairness of these happenings.....life is full of disappointments, as they say.

Looking back at my own, more modest service as a torpedo-man, and at those beastly weapons themselves, for which I had been an essential 'cog in the wheel' for maintaining, and firing, it was comforting to know that I never had the occasion to fire one ' in anger', to quite possibly cause the death of those on whatever vessel was at the receiving end, but of course should such an action have occurred, this after all was our raison d'etre. I am proud that of all those many torpedoes I had fired, either at targets or when just set to run and then be recovered, not one was lost to malfunction. Perhaps that was because every torpedo that came aboard I checked over thoroughly. The torpedo officer of one submarine, not a qualified specialist in the branch, became slightly annoyed when I chose to do this. He pointed out they had only recently been serviced in the base workshops, and then became slightly irate when I said, "Yes but that could have been done by any Tom, Dick or Harry." Every torpedo I have launched would have my fingerprints all over it, because I was the one who had applied the final firing adjustments. The Mark 8 torpedo itself, just like the MG car I owned, was the 'Best of British' and considered so reliable, even after fifty-five years of service, that all those years later in 1982 (even with the more modern torpedoes available) it was the weapon of choice for the Commander of Courageous to use when targeting the Argentine cruiser General Belgrano.

I mulled over a number of employment options outside of the service, but my final decision was to carry on by supporting the Navy in a civilian role, which enabled me to remain in my home locality, doing what I believed to be worthwhile work for the next twenty-five years......but that's another story.

A new prince is born

I am now almost 94 years of age and am living alone. I am able to look after myself quite well, but without the support of my wonderful neighbours and friends I don't know quite where I would be, as I tend to be very forgetful now. My caring Italian-born friend, Maria, rings me about four times every day. She calls me because her physical disability prevents her from making the difficult journey to visit me. This would involve two bus-rides and a ferry crossing. She phones me to remind me to take my tablets and to check on what I am eating, but mainly I know it's because she wants to help break up my day and ease my sense of being alone. Her own life has been hard, her husband died while he was young which left her to bring up her children on her own. Credit is due to her to her that they have done well in life, and I am so pleased that they and their own children visit me still and regard me as being family.

I am blessed with kind and caring friends and my neighbours, Sylvia and Phil next door to me, and Margaret and Laurie, who live across the road. They help me in a multitude of ways, but especially with shopping and with hospital appointments.

I am living alone because the love of my life Beryl passed away in August 2004. She finally succumbed to that dreaded scourge of cancer after she suffered a fifteen-year cycle of flare-ups and remissions. The diagnosis came during that first five years of extreme grief for us, when our newly married, and very caring daughter Rebecca, was killed at the age of nineteen in an awful car accident.

To best describe Beryl, this tribute by Joan Russell of Friends of Gosport Museum (as published in their 2005 newsletter) will sum her up as well as any words that I can say:-

Beryl Peacey - Local historian, teacher and co-author

When Beryl's courageous battle with cancer ended on the 25th August 2004, the loss to her family and friends was shared by many sad circles within the Gosport community, not least by members of three societies, concerned with local history. The energy and determination with which she faced up to the disease and its remissions for over 15 years was applied equally to her contribution to Gosport's local history.

For 15 years she delighted mature students at St Vincent's College. She taught them how to explore the many historic buildings in our area, not just from books and maps, but on their own two feet, enjoying the expeditions she led so enthusiastically. The spin off for the St Vincent's local History Club, and the Friends of Gosport Museum, was a steady supply of well-informed recruits inter-linking at their meetings.

But it was as Secretary of the prestigious Gosport Society, for over twenty years, Beryl made her most lasting contribution. Without her intelligent and meticulous typing of the Society's minutes, letters and later publications might never have appeared in their present form. Her input, as co-researcher and co-author with Lesley Burton, on so many aspects of Gosport's local history is her finest legacy. It was so fitting that the booklet 'Wings over Gosport' published by the Gosport Society, in October 2004, is dedicated to the memory of Beryl Peacey.

Her tireless efforts, in support of `Teacher's Benevolent Fund', for the Gosport War Memorial Hospital and for Cancer Research, we miss now. Little wonder is it that Alverstoke Parish church was packed for the service which gave thanks for her life, for she gave so much, to so many.

We will remember Beryl's last brave appearance at the veteran's D- Day parade and memorial service in June 2004. Impeccably dressed, as always, she turned out to support her heroic husband Chris, looking as though a puff of wind might blow her away.

Goodbye dear Beryl, thank you, and God bless you.

Joan Russell

This has been an eventful year so far... some events bad, others good. Probably the worst day was when my car was stolen from where I had parked it in Gosport. If this has ever happened to you, then you will understand the stress and doubt it involves. You doubt yourself, perhaps I had mistaken where I thought I had parked the car. I searched every street in the locality, twice. Then after the tiring and fruitless search I had the long walk home, thinking as I walked, that some would think I had simply forgotten where I had parked the car.... others might think I shouldn't be driving at my age anyway. As it turned out I was supported by all around me, including the police. My car, which for years I had kept in pristine condition, was eventually found in a local street where it had been abandoned. It was in such an awful state it was later declared a write-off for insurance purposes. Although I was paid the car's insurance value, it has now put an end to that measure of independence that the car gave me.

Some of the brighter events include when BBC 'South Today' reporter, Steve Humphrey, filmed an interview with me with regard to the forthcoming naming ceremony for the new aircraft carrier HMS Prince of Wales. Excerpts of it were shown on that evening's programme and on Forces TV News a few days later. It seems I am the only living survivor of the sinking by the Japanese of the battleship after which she is named.

Shortly after that, on the 7th September 2017, the Navy sent a petty officer to escort me by air to Rosyth, Scotland, from where I could attend the naming of the ship the following day. Unfortunately, despite my request, I was not provided with photographs taken on the day, so I have nothing tangible to remind me of that event. It makes me wonder if any of those eminent dignitaries present, Prince Charles, the Duchess of Cornwall and the first Sea Lord, etc., would receive photographs if they had requested them. Not to worry though, perhaps I will live long enough Bob so you and I can go aboard her when she comes into Portsmouth! "I will dig out my bosun's whistle and pipe you aboard" said I.

POSTSCRIPT

Chris was destined not to hold a copy of this book in his hand and that fact would not have troubled him. Knowing his sense of humour, as I do, it would probably have amused him. Chris passed away on the 24th March 2018.

Audio tapes of his Service experience had been lodged with the Imperial War Museum back in the 1980s but he looked on this book to be a means of recording more detailed events and interesting people he had met and served with during his life journey, and to be 'out there' even after he had crossed the bar, for whoever might be interested, and perhaps cause them to reflect on those precious and often amusing little happenings which make life worthwhile.

Chris's funeral was held on St Georges Day 23rd April 2018 which I think is fitting for a man who had more than proved his patriotism; his final voyage under the White Ensign was saluted by Standard Bearers of the Ganges Association Solent Division and the Gosport Branch of the Submariners Association and many members of both organisations as well as a Lt Commander and three crew-members of the aircraft carrier Prince of Wales, lastly, but certainly not the least, were many of his friends and neighbours who had cared for him to the end.

Chris Peacey's original oil-painting of the battleship Prince of Wales has been presented by me, on behalf of Chris, to the aircraft carrier Prince of Wales. The painting will hang in a place of honour in the Warrant Officers and Chief Petty Officers mess